D0398553

Slightly Chipped

Also by the Goldstones

Used and Rare: Travels in the Book World

Lawrence Goldstone

Rights
Offline

Nancy Goldstone

Trading Up: Surviving Success as a Woman Trader on Wall Street
Bad Business: A Novel
Mommy and the Murder
Money and the Money

Slightly Chipped

Footnotes in Booklore

Lawrence
and
Nancy Goldstone

St. Martin's Press New York

THOMAS DUNNE BOOKS.
An imprint of St. Martin's Press.

Material written under the byline of Lawrence and/or Nancy Goldstone appears in abbreviated form in Chapters 5, 7, and 9 and was first published in *Biblio*.

Library of Congress Cataloging-in-Publication Data

Goldstone, Lawrence.
Slightly chipped : footnotes in booklore / Lawrence and Nancy Goldstone. — 1st ed.
p. cm.
"Thomas Dunne books."
ISBN: 0-312-20587-2
1. Book collecting—New England. 2. Book collecting—Middle Atlantic States. 3. Goldstone, Lawrence. 4. Goldstone, Nancy Bazelon. I. Goldstone, Nancy Bazelon. II. Title.
Z987.5.U6G64 1999
002'.075—dc21 99-18058
CIP

First Edition: May 1999

10 9 8 7 6 5 4 3 2 1

For Emily, who loves to read

Slightly Chipped

CHAPTER 1

It was the first Friday in May 1997, and we were in Boston for the Fifth Annual Spring Antiquarian Book Fair.

Usually when we are in Boston, even for a fair, we make the rounds of the used-book stores. On this visit, however, we intended to make the rounds of the *new*-book stores. Our book, *Used and Rare: Travels in the Book World,* had just come out, and there is nothing quite like seeing your shiny new book sitting there on the shelves.

We weren't Stephen King—we didn't expect to see waist-high stacks of *Used and Rare* clogging the aisles or crowds of screaming fanatics fighting over that one last copy. However, since some significant sections of *Used and Rare* had been set in Boston and were devoted to some of the city's more distinguished rare-book dealers, we felt confident that, at least here, booksellers would have ordered a few copies. In our wildest fantasies, there might even be a small stack in the window—four or five books maybe. We dreamed of an assistant manager's eyes going wide in recognition as we walked through the door. He would say: "Aren't you the Goldstones? I loved your book. See, we put them right in the window. Would you mind signing them for us?"

As a result, we had gotten in early and saved the better part of the day to meander about. We started in Back Bay at the giant mall off Boylston Street. Walking slowly to savor the moment, we headed to Doubleday. When we got there, we paused, then held hands and walked in.

We checked the books displayed up front. *Used and Rare* was not among them. Oh, well, we hadn't *really* expected to be in the front anyway. New nonfiction would be just fine, so we strolled over there. *Used and Rare* wasn't in new nonfiction either.

Trying to look casual, we checked every shelf, including juvenile literature. No books.

Hmm.

"Well, this is a small store."

"Yeah, they have hardly anything. Just best-sellers."

"Yeah. There's another bookstore in this mall. I think it's a Rizzoli. They'll have a better selection."

"Right."

So we walked on to Rizzoli. We were still holding hands, but the grips had gotten a little tighter.

Rizzoli was a very handsome store and, as we suspected, seemed to favor a more literary selection than Doubleday. Prominently featured was *A History of Reading* by Alberto Manguel, which had been published about six months earlier to glowing though not widespread reviews. If they still had that book on the shelves, maybe they would have ours.

The new nonfiction section was in the center of the store and consisted of about one hundred books, but *Used and Rare* was not one of them.

We left the mall and made our way to Waterstone on Exeter Street. Our aspirations had now been reduced to just seeing a copy of our book anywhere, and of all the anywheres, Waterstone seemed the best shot. It was a huge, three-storied, twenty-thousand-square-foot store that occupied an entire building and seemed to have everything ever published in any language.

We went up the stairs to the main floor, where literally hundreds of titles of new nonfiction were on display. We examined both by title and by author, just in case we had been misfiled. Nothing. We went over to fiction, just in case they didn't know we'd written a memoir. Nothing.

"I'm going to ask."

"No, Larry, don't."

"I'm going to."

So we walked over to the information desk—one purposefully, one lagging back a bit, trying to look inconspicuous. The information desk was presided over by two men and two women, each of whom looked to be a sophomore English major at one of the local colleges.

"Excuse me."

"Yes?" It was one of the young women. She had long brown hair pulled straight back, no makeup, and a lot of earrings in one ear.

"Do you have a book called *Used and Rare*?"

"Who's the author?"

"Uhhh—Goldstone, I think."

She went to her computer. "Yes, we have it. It's on the third floor. It's alllll the way in the back." She gave one long wave with her hand to indicate just how far in the back that was. "You'll have to ask someone when you get up there. Tell them you want literary criticism."

"Literary criticism?"

"It's where we put all the books we don't know what else to do with." She shrugged and smiled. "We call it the garbage dump of the store," she added cheerfully.

After a more subdued lunch than we had anticipated, we decided to visit the Museum of Fine Arts instead of any more bookstores. Then, at about a quarter after four, we headed off toward downtown. (One of the great things about Boston is that it's small enough so that almost everything is within walking distance.) The fair was being held in the Park Plaza Castle, which is a genuine castle on the corner of Arlington Street and Columbus Avenue. The doors were supposed to open at five. We got there with about ten minutes to spare.

It had been a warm afternoon, and since it seems to be a rule that book fairs must be held in stuffy, overheated halls, we were dressed in light clothes, expecting to just walk right in. As we neared the castle, however, we saw a large crowd of people near the front door—something of a surprise for a regional book fair. But there was a lot more than that. The whole place was lit up by huge spotlights in the street. There were trucks, police cars with flashing lights, and people walking around talking frantically into walkie-talkies. Dominating the scene was a crane with a large bucket on the end. The bucket was being held level with a window that had been removed on the top floor of the castle. A man was inside the bucket, and three spotlights were directed right at him. It was almost as if the guy were threatening to jump and they were lighting him up in preparation for Mel Gibson to come and try to talk him out of it.

We looked at each other.

"Can this be for the fair?"

"What else would they be doing up there? They must be covering it for local television."

"Covering a book fair?"

"I told you books were catching on."

As we got closer, we could see that the crowd consisted of two distinct components. The first was comprised of members of the film crew. They were men and women who looked exactly alike—

hip black clothes, leather jackets, baseball hats, and holster belts for their walkie-talkies slung low, gunfighter style. None was over thirty. The other segment was the book-collecting crowd. They were also men and women who looked exactly alike but in this case they wore rumpled clothing, tousled long hair, and glasses. Almost no one in this group was under thirty.

The book collectors seemed to have made a focus of a very large, sullen, extremely Irish Boston police officer who had set himself up as a human barricade between the street and the entrance to the Park Plaza Castle. No one was getting by, and this was making the book buyers frantic. Each was apparently convinced that a competitor had somehow slipped inside and was greedily snapping up the very books that he or she had come here to purchase. As a result, the police officer was being badgered unmercifully, with sentences that began, "*Pleeease.* You don't understand. You *have* to let me in because . . ."—to which the police officer, an impassive twenty-year veteran of Boston political demonstrations, responded not at all.

There was a woman standing next to us who, by the frustration etched on her face, had obviously been there for some time.

"What's going on?" we asked.

"They're filming a commercial," she said, practically spitting out the words. "They're not going to let anyone in until the crane comes down."

"A commercial? For the book fair?"

She gave us a strange look and gestured with her thumb. "For the mattress store across the street," she said.

A half hour later, after the film crew had gotten all their equipment and mattresses into the top floor of the castle and the temperature had dropped by at least twenty degrees, we were finally allowed to go into the fair. Along with the rest of the herd of muttering bibliophiles, we shivered our way to the front door, paid our $6 apiece for tickets, and trudged into the hall.

The second we were inside, everything changed. We forgot how long we had waited, how cold we were, even that we hadn't seen our book in the stores. We had just entered a large room filled with wonderful books. We even held hands again.

Unlike the Boston *International* Antiquarian Book Fair, which is held in November in the prestigious Hynes Auditorium, and which is sponsored by the Antiquarian Booksellers Association of America (ABAA), the Boston *Spring* Antiquarian Book Fair is sponsored by Mariab, which stands for Massachusetts and Rhode Island Antiquarian Booksellers Inc. (Why they left off the last letter of the acronym is a mystery, unless they decided that "Mariabi" sounded too much like a board game or a Latin dance.) Although there is some overlap between the Mariab membership and that of the ABAA, Mariab, in addition to being regional, is largely comprised of dealers whose prices top out in the hundreds of dollars instead of in the thousands.

This makes for a distinct difference in the atmosphere of the respective fairs. The ABAA fair, like its sister, the New York Antiquarian Book Fair, is filled with treasures. One year in New York, for example, we saw a pristine 1687 first edition of Sir Isaac Newton's *Philosophiae naturalis principia mathematica*—which means the mathematical principles of natural philosophy, by the way—for $210,000. (A very reasonable price, according to the dealer, and he must have been right because it was snapped up immediately.) We've seen Dickens in parts, *Gulliver's Travels,* first editions of Tocqueville, and other of the great books of the world, all in the best possible condition. It is awe-inspiring to walk up and down the aisles seeing one museum piece after another.

But museums induce respectful silence. When you walk through the Hynes or the Seventh Regiment Armory, where the New York fair is held, you step gingerly, and when you do reach for a book, it is with exaggerated care and under the sharp eye of an often stern dealer dressed in a jacket and tie.

By contrast, the Mariab fair is more like a party, convivial and intimate. The noise hits you instantly. The fair-goers tend to be younger, and everyone is more casually dressed. People walk around eating, chatting each other up, ribbing each other. You'll find one dealer sitting at another's booth, and he'll say, "Oh, his stuff isn't any good. Come over to my booth."

But most importantly, the books are more accessible to people like us. We've always found something at this fair for which we'd been searching for a long time, like *The Death Ship* by B. Traven or a 1929 edition of *Dracula,* at a price we could afford. As a dealer friend of ours told us, "Mariab is always interesting. It's the first big fair of the spring, and you never know just what the dealers have squirreled away during the winter."

In our first five minutes of walking the aisles, we saw that this fair was going to be first-rate as well. There was, as always, an eclectic selection of modern firsts, Americana, detective fiction, occult fiction, interesting dust jackets, cookbooks, art books, photography, and avant-garde literature. We wandered through for awhile without even thinking about buying anything, just sucking up the mood and stopping occasionally to chat with old friends.

"Hi," said John Sanderson, a tall, thin golf addict with brown hair and a mustache who had always evoked the image of a Shakespearean scholar, which, in fact, he was. Since we'd moved from the Berkshires to Connecticut, we no longer saw John regularly.

"How's the book doing?" he asked.

"Oh . . . great."

He wagged a finger at us. "Don't forget," he said, "I want to play myself in the movie."

We walked a little further, and Rusty Mott came up to us. Rusty ran Howard S. Mott Rare Books in Sheffield, Massachusetts. It was he who had showed us the weathered copy of *The Works* by Sir William Davenant, in which Herman Melville had taken notes in preparation for writing *Moby Dick,* and who had sold us a pamphlet about the American Revolution.

"Hi," we said. "Are you exhibiting here?"

"No," he said. "I love this fair. I just come to look. Say, how's the book doing?"

"Oh, its doing just . . . great."

After Rusty, we decided that if we wanted to have any fun at this fair, it might be best to try and avoid people we knew. That turned out to be a good idea, and we were able to amble about blissfully and anonymously for about an hour. We hadn't really bought anything, just a twenty-dollar first edition of Laurie Colwin's *Home Cooking*. Then we came upon a booth toward the far wall on the left, near the front. It was one of the smaller displays, only three or four shelves high, set on tables arranged in an L-shape. The sign said, "ON THE ROAD BOOKS," with the name of a town in Connecticut that we had never heard of underneath.

We had seen this stall before on our first go-through, but we had assumed that the owner had named his shop after the Kerouac novel and that therefore On The Road Books specialized in Beat literature. Beat literature is okay, but not one of our favorites, so we hadn't stopped to look. But this time we did stop, and the second we did, we saw that this booth was going to be special. The books were all remarkably crisp and clear and bright. It was modern literature, and the selection seemed to have been picked out just for us. If we'd had enough money, we would have simply gotten a very large box and transferred the entire display to our library. Then, we noticed one particular book on the top shelf.

"Is that a *Mrs. Bridge*?"

Mrs. Bridge was written by Evan S. Connell, Jr., and published in 1959. Both *Mrs. Bridge* and its companion book, *Mr. Bridge,* published ten years later, were taken very closely from Mr. Connell's own upbringing in a suburb of Kansas City. Set primarily during the 1930s and 1940s, these novels detail the lives of India and Walter Bridge, an upper-middle-class couple, and Ruth, Douglas, and Carolyn, their three children.

Despite a sizable cult following, *Mrs. Bridge* and *Mr. Bridge* have never been fully recognized for the masterpieces of American realism that they are. Both novels are written in spare, deceptively gentle prose and presented as a string of loosely related vignettes. (*Mrs. Bridge* alone has over one hundred chapters, some less than a page long.) They are, all the same, devastating portraits of American suburbia and of the bankruptcy of values and futility of existence of those who live there. Each is every bit as mesmerizing in its way as were *Babbitt* or the works of John O'Hara in theirs.

For example, in *Mrs. Bridge,* the chapter entitled "Frozen Fruit" begins:

> With Ruth gone and with Carolyn at home only an occasional week end, with Mr. Bridge continuing to spend long hours at the office, and with Douglas appearing only for meals, Mrs. Bridge found the days growing interminable; she could not remember when a day had seemed so long since the infinite hours of childhood, and so she began casting about rueful and disconsolate for some way to occupy the time. There were mornings when she lay in bed wide awake until noon, afraid to get up because there was nothing to do. She knew Harriet would take care of ordering the groceries, Harriet would take care of everything, Harriet somehow was running the house and Mrs. Bridge had the dismal sensation of knowing that she, herself, could leave town for a week and perhaps no one would get overly excited.

She only does get up when she remembers that Mr. Bridge told her to get the car washed and waxed, but, upon emerging from the bedroom with this announcement, is informed by Harriet that the chore had already been performed the previous Saturday.

> "Are you sure?" asked Mrs. Bridge.
> Harriet nodded.

> "Oh. Well, then," she said doubtfully, "I suppose it doesn't need to be done again. Isn't that strange? He must have forgotten to tell me." She noticed Harriet looking at her without expression, but intently, and she became embarrassed. She dropped the car keys back in her purse and slowly took off her hat. She had driven the Lincoln several times since Saturday and it was odd she had not noticed the difference.

Ever more desperate for something to do, Mrs. Bridge finally finds a friend who is as bored as she. The friend agrees to come over. They spend the afternoon drinking coffee (made by Harriet) at the kitchen table, discussing a variety of topics of local interest; for example, that because an increasing number of young men are enlisting to fight in the war, delivery service at the Piggly-Wiggly has deteriorated. Finally, around four o'clock, they decide they are hungry.

> They went to the kitchen and Mrs. Bridge looked into the refrigerator.
>
> "Strawberries and whipped cream?" she suggested. "These are frozen, of course. They don't really taste the same as the fresh, but they certainly are a time-saver."

But perhaps the most compelling aspect of the Bridges is their timelessness. If you substitute Range Rovers for Lincolns and cell phones for kitchen gadgets and frozen foods, the books might just as easily have been written last year instead of decades ago. The social inbreeding and the tortured vanity of the suburbs that were—and are—so distinctly American have never been so perfectly depicted as in these books. And, of course, they are an indication that, technology notwithstanding, we haven't progressed so very far at all.

A few years ago, Merchant and Ivory made a film version of

both novels called *Mr. and Mrs. Bridge,* starring Mr. and Mrs. Paul Newman. It was a decent and respectful effort, but the power and relentless grip of the books were sadly absent. We have often lamented that few who saw the film would be inspired to go out and read the infinitely superior books.

We pulled out the *Mrs. Bridge* from the On The Road display. It had a dust jacket that we had never seen before—white, with a pen-and-ink drawing of a woman of about sixty with a string of pearls around her neck, a tiny mouth set in a tight smile, and a benign, vacant expression on her face. In the background was a conservatively furnished drawing room done in olive and orange watercolor. The woman seemed to be daydreaming in the general direction of a tea table to her left, upon which sat an orange telephone. We turned to the spine and saw the name Heinemann, which we knew to be a British publisher.

"It's the first U.K.," said the dealer, a large man with a small crewcut, sitting in a folding chair next to the booth. "The dust jacket is much more interesting than the American, don't you think?"

We did think. The dust jacket to the American edition had a dull gold background, with three paper dolls representing the children in white silhouette in the foreground, with another tea table, upon which were placed a black telephone and a shocking pink hat and white gloves. A vague drawing of the Lincoln is behind the table, and across the top of the front cover is a place card with the words "Mrs. Bridge" in script. The spine is the same dull gold as the cover, with the title placed in a rectangle colored in the same pink as the hat. There is a pink fan underneath.

Although the book did not have a large printing, it is the use of this pink that makes a first American edition of *Mrs. Bridge* in good condition sell for well over two hundred dollars. That is because the pink is notoriously susceptible to fading, so the color on the spine almost never matches the color on the telephone. *Mr. Bridge,* on the other hand, had a much larger printing (and in nonfading colors) and is generally available for under fifty dollars.

We knew a lot about *Mrs. Bridge.* It was one of the first books we had thought of when the idea of our own library began to take shape. We had searched for it, with no success at all, for over three years.

Then, in the most unlikely of bookshops . . .

We had just moved to Connecticut, and, thrown in with the new home, at no extra charge, was a whole new Yellow Pages section of "Book Dealers—Used & Rare" to go through. A quick scan revealed that the closest dealer to us was Kemet Books in Fairfield. It is often hard to tell, just from the listing, what kind of a selection a dealer offers. Sometimes the best (or most-expensive) books are found at dealers who place the least-ostentatious ads. Whoever owned Kemet Books had paid for just the phone number, although he or she had also sprung to have it in capitals and boldface.

We called and got a recording. It was a man's voice, declarative, making no attempt to be clever or cheerful, noting that the shop dealt in used and rare books, special publications, and ephemera and was open Wednesday through Saturday, noon through 6 P.M., but to call if you were coming from a long distance.

Since we were only coming from the next town, the following Wednesday at two o'clock we got into the car and drove through Fairfield and found Kemet Books just before Bridgeport, on the bottom floor of a small, light brown frame house, across the street from Three Brothers Pizza and a vacant shopping center, and just down the road from Drotos Brothers Hungarian Imports & Specialties. There was a little yard, with nothing in it, surrounded by a chain-link fence (in front) and with an American flag hanging from the porch. Kemet Books was on the ground floor and shared the building with Teltronics Engineering and Emil & Tom Grega Painters, who occupied an out-building to the right.

As soon as we got out of the car, we noticed that a sign on the front door read, CLOSED. We walked up and knocked, just in case the dealer had forgotten to change the sign, but it was dark inside, and there was no response.

The next day we called first. A man picked up on the third ring. It was the same voice as was on the answering machine.

"Hello?" he said.

"Is this Kemet Books?"

"Who's calling?"

Who's calling? "Uh, you don't know me. My wife and I are collectors, and we came by yesterday . . ."

"I wasn't here yesterday."

"Right. We saw that."

"I don't usually come in on Wednesdays."

"Are you open today?"

"I'll be here until about five. Are you going to come by?"

"Yes. We'll be there in about an hour."

"What's your name?"

"Larry Goldstone."

This response was evidently satisfactory. "Okay," he said and hung up.

We repeated our drive from the day before and came to the same house. This time the sign on the door read, OPEN.

We pushed the door open. Directly in front of us was a dark narrow staircase, which we assumed led up to Teltronics. To our right was another door. We went in and found ourselves in a small room, about fifteen by twelve, facing a bookcase loaded with old cookbooks, books on art and photography, and a group called "Ancient Civilizations."

"Looking for anything in particular?" The voice came from a man coming though a doorway at the opposite end of the shop. We could see that the room from which he had emerged was even smaller than the one we were now in. This second room was cramped and dimly lit, with hardly space enough for a desk amid the piles and piles of books. There was, however, a tiny television propped up on milk crates.

The man himself was in his forties. He was short and round, wearing a white short-sleeved shirt and a dark vest, but no tie. Although we had half expected to be asked for a password, he was completely hospitable. He had an odd way about him, though. He managed to be cheerful and morose at the same time.

"Uh, no. We'd just like to look around."

"Okay," he replied. "But I have a number of items that aren't on the shelves."

"Thank you." The fiction and mystery sections were in a little alcove to the left, and although the shelves and carpet were dingy, the books looked interesting. We immediately noted a number of titles by Steinbeck, Edna Ferber, John O'Hara, and, in mystery, Elmore Leonard and John Le Carré.

"Are these all firsts?"

"There are a lot of firsts there," replied the man, "but I keep my better items over here," and he gestured with his right hand to a bookcase next to the wall that abutted the office.

We took a step in that direction as he removed a book from the upper-left-hand corner of the bookcase. It was pale blue and was encased in a cellophane bag.

"If this had a dust jacket," he said, "it would be worth about eight thousand dollars."

He held it out for us to look at. It was F. Scott Fitzgerald's first book, *This Side of Paradise*. It looked to be in good condition.

"What are you selling it for without the dust jacket?"

"I'm willing to let it go for twelve hundred fifty," he said. "I'm trying to get money together to do a new catalog."

We nodded.

"If I keep it," he continued, "I'm going to make a clamshell case for it and make the outside of the case look just like the dust jacket."

"That's a good idea," we said.

"Are you sure you are not looking for anything in particular? I have a lot of things in the back that I haven't put out yet. I'm planning on doing a catalog as soon as I can buy some new software."

"No, that's all right, we'll just look," and we turned back to the alcove.

There weren't a lot of books there, and while nothing was extraordinary, the selection was surprisingly good, and the prices were reasonable. In the O'Haras, for example, there was a first edition of *And Other Stories* for $30 and one of *The Big Laugh* for $35. Both were in excellent condition. In the Le Carrés, there was a first U.K. of *Smiley's People,* also in first-class condition, for $50. There was a first edition, second issue of Steinbeck's *The Moon Is Down* for only $45. The used books were good, too.

"You haven't been in here before, have you?"

We turned around, and he was standing there, not so much watching us as waiting to renew the conversation.

"No."

"Just visiting?"

"We just moved here."

"How did you find me?"

"We looked in the Yellow Pages."

He stood there expectantly.

"You have very nice books here."

"Thank you. I can't afford to compete with the big dealers, so I try to get a good selection in good condition and sell them for a little less than anyone else does."

"We don't remember seeing your shop listed in the Connecticut Antiquarian Booksellers Directory," we said. The directory is a thin, blue, letter-envelope-size pamphlet with listings of sixty dealers from all across the state that we had seen at book fairs. "Do you advertise there?"

"No. They wanted two hundred dollars." The man said this with a tone of moral outrage, as if the publishers had demanded that he sell his wife and children into slavery in order to have his business listed in the Connecticut Antiquarian Booksellers Directory.

"Do you display at the fairs?" In addition to regional fairs, we had noted that there was a book fair held right in Fairfield each November.

"I used to, but they charge too much. I can't afford it."

We tried turning back to look at the books again, but the man was indefatigable.

"Are you sure there's nothing special you're looking for?" he asked.

Browsing being hopeless, we thought hard.

"How about . . . a . . . first edition . . . of . . . *Mrs. Bridge*?"

He nodded. "I've got that," he said.

"You *do?*" Up until then, we had never even seen a first of *Mrs. Bridge.*

He nodded. "Would you like to have a look at it?"

"We'd love to."

He disappeared into the back room, and when he reemerged, sure enough, there was *Mrs. Bridge.*

He handed it to us. There was some fading to the pink on the spine, and there was some minor foxing to the back cover, but it was generally in good condition, certainly what would be described in a catalog as "near fine."

We opened to the front endpaper, where most dealers pencil in their prices. The endpaper was blank.

"How much is this?"

"I put my prices on the rear endpaper," he said. "I think it's one eighty."

"Ooh, one eighty, that's a little high," we said. At that time we had no idea what a first edition of *Mrs. Bridge* actually went for.

The man seemed to spend some time in thought. "Well," he said finally, "you look like you'll be good customers, and I really need money now, so I can let you have it for one fifty."

Although we had no specific idea of the actual value of the book, just the fact that we hadn't seen it once in our three years of searching was enough. It was obviously a hard book to get.

"We'll take it."

The man then proceeded to enter into the most scrupulous invoicing process we had ever seen. First, he took out a clear lucite clipboard with a metal clip, on which were alternating white and yellow 8 × 10 preprinted invoices. The man squeezed open the clip, carefully aligned a piece of carbon paper between the top two sheets, then reclosed the clip. He picked up a pen, but before he wrote, he looked up.

"I'd love to have a computer system that did billing," he said.

He opened to the rear endpaper. There, under the notation, "1st, 1959, author's second book," was a twelve-digit entry, a combination of letters and numbers. He filled in an invoice number (6049), the date, and the name and address of the customer (that was us). Underneath were three columns: description, inventory number, and price. Under description he wrote, "Mrs. Bridge." He lifted the top sheet and the carbon paper, copied the twelve digits on to his (yellow) copy of the invoice, then took out an eraser and carefully erased the entry in the book. His pencil entry was so lightly done that when he was finished erasing, it was impossible to detect that a figure had ever been there in the first place. After that, he painstakingly realigned the carbon paper. For price, he wrote, "$180." We were just about to protest when underneath on a blank line he wrote "Spec Disc" and then wrote, "($30)." He then subtotaled the two figures and added the tax.

This process took about five minutes. "How long have you had the shop?" we asked. If he ever had a crowd in there, he'd have a lot of trouble with throughput.

"Six years," he replied.

"What did you do before?"

"I was an accountant," he said.

Now, a mere six months later, at the On The Road booth, we were confronted with another *Mrs. Bridge*. We checked the price: $125.

According to the rules as noted in *ABC for Book Collectors,* a collector is always supposed to "follow the flag" that is, collect the edition from the publisher of the author's nationality even if a foreign edition may have been published first, although this rule has some flexibility as many dealers will, if they can get away with it, list, say, a British first by an American author as "preceding the American" and charge accordingly.

But whatever the provenance, the U.K. edition of *Mrs. Bridge* had a much more interesting dust jacket than the American, and it was in near-perfect condition. More than that, even though the American edition was technically more valuable, the U.K. edition was unusual and a more eclectic choice for our library. After all, how many first editions could Connell have sold in the U.K.? At the time, he was obscure here.

We stood, holding the book, silently debating. The dealer, in very undealerlike fashion, sat patiently and let us think, making no attempt to sell.

Finally, one of us said to the other, "Let's put it down for a minute and look at the other books."

We put *Mrs. Bridge* down on a table on the side and started to browse. Immediately we saw, next to the empty space from which we had removed *Mrs. Bridge, The Anatomy Lesson and other stories.* This was Connell's first book. This also had a striking dust jacket, an etching in white on a dark olive green background of a nude woman posing as if for an artist, with a skull in the foreground. This was also a first U.K. in near-perfect condition.

"I wonder if these stories are any good?" Connell tends to be uneven. Some of his later work was not nearly up to the standard of the Bridges.

"Oh, they're excellent." It was the dealer, speaking for the first time.

We turned. He had said it in such a way that we knew he was speaking as a reader. We took him in. He was kind of bearlike, but exuded an earnestness and gentleness that were incongruous with his size and shape.

"How do you get these books in such great condition?"

"I don't buy that many books," he said, "but it is important to me to sell only books that are in really good condition." He paused. "I often like first U.K. editions better than American. Here, this one is unusual, too." He reached over and extracted a book from the shelf behind him. It was *Tender Is the Night.* The dust jacket was a charcoal gray drawing of a man walking down a city street at night, wearing a top hat and an obviously expensive overcoat over evening dress, smoking a cigarette.

We opened the book. It had been published in 1953 by Grey Walls Press, and on the title page it read, "*With the author's final revisions and a preface by* MALCOLM COWLEY." We already had *Tender Is the Night,* and with the same revisions and preface, but ours was a Scribner's U.S. edition with a plain buff, not particularly attractive dust jacket. Nor was ours in anywhere near this condition.

We opened both *The Anatomy Lesson* and *Tender Is the Night* to the front endpaper. Each was $85.

We put these down next to, but not on top of, *Mrs. Bridge,* and turned back to the shelves.

"Look, Larry, *The Prime of Miss Jean Brodie.* I always wanted this."

"That's funny," said the dealer with a small smile. "That just happens to be a first U.S., but I have a first U.K. back at the shop."

The Prime of Miss Jean Brodie was $50.

"How much is the first U.K.?" we asked.

"One twenty-five," he said.

The Prime of Miss Jean Brodie went down next to, but not on top of, *Tender Is the Night* and *The Anatomy Lesson.*

"That's enough!"

"Okay, what do we do?"

"Which one can you live without?"

"I can definitely live without the first U.K. of *The Prime of Miss Jean Brodie,*" one of us said virtuously. "The first American will be fine."

"Very good, Nancy. That's a start. And we really should have *The Anatomy Lesson.*"

"Right. And *Mrs. Bridge* is out of the question. We're not going to spend a hundred and twenty-five dollars on a book we already own."

"Right. It's too bad, though. What a great dust jacket."

"Yeah, I love it, too. That leaves *Tender Is the Night.*"

"Well, we can always get another edition of *Tender Is the Night* to replace ours, but not like this one. This is striking."

"I suppose so, and since we're not getting *Mrs. Bridge* . . ."

As one, we turned to the dealer.

"If we took all three—" we offered coyly.

He thought for a moment. "I'll give you the dealer discount," he said. "That's twenty percent."

"Thank you," we said gratefully.

Unusual for us after spending this much money, there was not even a hint of hesitation or regret. The three books were clearly worth it.

As he was writing up an invoice, we found our gaze traveling magnetically back to *Mrs. Bridge,* still sitting there on the desk. Suddenly, an idea dawned.

"We have a first U.S. Would you be willing to swap the first U.K. for it?"

"What kind of condition is it in?" the dealer asked.

We described our copy and also noted that we had paid $150 for it.

"Sure," he said. "I'm willing to do that if you are."

We looked at each other. "What do you think?"

"Oh, I don't know."

"Why don't you do this," said the dealer. "Take this copy home with you and decide what you want to do. Then you can either send this copy back to me, or you can send me yours."

"Really? Do you want us to give you a deposit?"

"No, that's okay."

We were both so surprised, all we could come up with was: "Wow, thanks."

He handed us an invoice for the three books, and we wrote him a check. He looked down at the check once we had handed it over.

"You're the Goldstones?" he said. "I just finished reading your book. A friend of mine gave it to me as a gift. He said, 'You're going to love this.' And I did." He stood up for the first time and stuck out his hand.

We felt big, grateful, dopey smiles pass across our faces as we shook hands in turn.

Thus began our friendship with Kevin Rita.

We took the first U.K. *Mrs. Bridge* home and put it on the top shelf of our new, built-in bookcase, next to the first American. When we started to reach to take the first American down from the shelf, our hands stopped working.

"We're not going to send it back, are we?"

"No."

"And we're not going to send back the first U.K. either, are we?"

"No."

"We're going to send him a check and keep both, aren't we?"

"Yes."

When we called Kevin to tell him he wasn't getting the first American, just in case he had a customer, he said, "Oh, I didn't say anything, but I thought you'd end up keeping both."

"How did you know?"

"Well, I can usually tell a lot about the people who buy books from me. You seemed to love your books just like I do, and that's what I would have done."

Chapter 2

It was 8:40 in the morning—humid, overcast, late July. Only twenty minutes to go. Movement was stiff, conversation forced. Occasionally, men or women glanced uneasily at the barricades that soon would be the focal point of their headlong charge. In the battle to come, neighbors would become combatants, close friends sworn enemies.

It was the opening day of the Pequot Library sale.

Thousands of libraries across the country hold annual book sales, but not too many of these libraries are located in towns like Pequot. Pequot is in Connecticut, on the shore of Long Island Sound. It is quite small, part of Southport, which is, in turn, part of Fairfield. Although it is easy to be deceived by the quaint Native-American name, the average resident of Pequot has a net worth roughly equal to the gross national product of Nigeria. Don Imus used to live in Pequot, but he has since moved down the road to Westport, complaining that the residents were stuffy, and, besides, the light from the Pequot Yacht Club shined in his bedroom window.

The Pequot Library was built in the early 1890s, financed entirely by one local couple, Virginia and Elbert Monroe, in memory of Virginia's uncle. The Monroes were guided in this endeavor by the Reverend William H. Holman, a young, handsome, smooth-tongued, Harvard-educated minister who had come to the town only two years before and who liked to read.

The library the Monroes built was a sprawling, two-storied, Romanesque castle constructed from huge, rough-cut, salmon-colored granite blocks topped by an enormous roof made of terra-cotta tiles. There are hipped dormers in front and back, ribbon windows, and a seven-foot-high double oak door framed by an arcaded entrance porch. Inside, in addition to all the rooms that one would expect to find in a library, they built an auditorium with a seating capacity larger than the population of the town under a twenty-foot-high mahogany parquet cathedral ceiling. In the reading room is a working fireplace, which, for atmosphere, is kept well stoked in the winter. There is no moat, but the library is set back from Pequot Avenue by a half acre of scrupulously manicured lawn.

Over the years, in addition to its ordinary reference and circulation sections, the library has amassed a renowned rare book and genealogy collection that attracts scholars from across the nation. Part of the rare book collection is currently on loan to Yale—the only books in the Bienecke Library that are not owned by the university. In protest, the Yale librarians have refused to include these titles on their computerized listings.

Back in Pequot, that part of the collection available to the general public is kept in a large room on the main floor. The shelves are of handcrafted wrought iron decorated in an intricate fleur-de-lis pattern. The ceiling is made entirely of thick, frosted glass tiles, which serve as the floor of the room above. At the end of the main passageway, catching the rays of the sun, are three extremely valuable Tiffany stained-glass windows. The center panel depicts William Caxton, publisher, in 1474, of the first book printed in English, standing next to Aldus Manutius the Elder, the famed Venetian printer and inventor of italics, whose pocket-size editions made the written word available to the common man. The Tree of Knowledge spreads out behind them.

To prepare the library for its annual sale, an army of frail-looking, white-haired volunteers wearing lots of plaid (women on the top, men on the bottom) had worked the entire year to sort and classify books that had been donated by the box-load by people from all over the area. During the last two weeks before the sale, the auditorium had been cleared and two enormous tents pitched on the lawn to the right of the building. In addition to procuring coffee machines and coercing baked goods out of their neighbors, the volunteer force had hauled the ninety-five thousand books said to comprise this year's sale up from the basement on the dumbwaiter and then spread them out on the long tables that had been set up in each sale area. To repel incursions by overeager book buyers, the local Boy Scout troop had been enlisted to sleep overnight in the tents.

The sale was to run for three days. From nine o'clock until noon on this, the first day, all books would be double the little price penciled in on the front endpaper. From noon Friday, and all day Saturday, the books would be sold at the penciled price. On Sunday, any remaining books would be free.

When we got to Pequot, we found the normally deserted streets packed with cars. There were even policemen directing traffic, the only uniformed presence we had ever seen in the town other than on the Fourth of July. Although there were one or two available parking spots deceptively close to the library, we strongly suspected these to be sucker plays and so ended up parking near the train station, about a half mile away. As we were hiking back, we saw a shiny red convertible carefully maneuver into one of the nearby spots. Sure enough, as soon as the occupant had gotten out of the car and hurried toward the library, a Fairfield policeman sidled over and wrote out a big, fat, Pequot-size parking ticket.

When we got to the lawn, there were well over three hundred people milling about. On a smaller lawn this might have seemed crowded.

The difference between most of these three hundred people and the average Pequot resident was immediately apparent. There was a woman in cowboy boots and a miniskirt so short as to be superfluous. There were men with unkempt beards and filthy baseball hats, women in T-shirts and Birkenstocks, and a lot of people of both sexes in short-sleeved button-down shirts and Dockers. They were armed with cardboard boxes or enormous shopping bags, sometimes as many as five or six apiece. The only thing missing on each of them was a little name tag that read, HI, I'M A BOOK DEALER.

Since we assumed the sale would not begin until somebody took down all those barricades in front of the doors and tents, we had some time to idle about. We had been idling about for five minutes when we saw a man holding a little orange ticket with a number on it.

"What's that?" we asked.

"They give out tickets to the first hundred people," he said.

This was news to us. There had been no announcement nor any indication that people were going to be admitted in any order whatever.

"Are there any more?" we asked. "Where did you get it?"

"Over by the front door. I don't know if they have any left," he said.

We walked up the steps. Three formidable, unsmiling septuagenarians sat behind a long table. They looked like judges at the Nuremberg trials.

"Uh—may we have a ticket?" we asked.

"Do you want the tent or the building?" asked the one in the middle.

"The tent, please." That was where the literature was.

"They're all gone," she said.

"Do you have any left for the building?"

Without answering, the woman on the end ripped off a little orange ticket from a roll and handed it to us. It had "92" printed on it.

At about ten to nine, people started to line up in some vague order of the number on their tickets. One or two even asked politely what number somebody else had, so that they didn't cut in front. For about five minutes, everyone chatted amiably with those in front of or behind them, discussing such things as this sale, previous sales, and how long it had taken them to drive here.

At about five to nine, a subtle creeping motion began. By three minutes to nine, the line had compressed to the extent that we, with our "92," found ourselves directly behind a woman who held "68."

Then conversation ceased and everybody began glancing alternately at their watch and the front door.

BOOM!

From some unknown quarter, the volunteers had dragged out a cannon and set it off. It was a very small cannon, so no one had noticed it, but it made a very big noise. Produced a good-size shock wave, too. It felt like someone had walked up and punched us in the chest. More than a few of our compatriots clutched at their hearts.

After everyone recovered from the blast, the realization set in that this must be the start of the sale. Initially, everyone remained polite, taking small, measured steps toward the door, careful not to move in front of the person ahead of them. Then the steps got faster. Then faster still. Within seconds, hundreds of dealers and a sprinkling of collectors (that was us) were stampeding through the door, elbows and cardboard boxes held high, all pretext of civilization abandoned.

We were unsure of the layout, so we paused just inside the door. Dealers streamed in around us, like white water surging past rocks.

The main auditorium was crammed with long tables divided by

categories, on which were heaped piles and piles of books. The entire floor space under the tables was filled with books as well. There were architecture, nature, world history, biography, classics, and the occult. On the stage of the auditorium, separated from the rest and removed from where children might wander, stood a table over which hung a sign that read EXOTICA, with the *x* crossed out and replaced with an *r*.

Over in the corner, just beyond the circulation desk, we saw a number of people swoop down on a table over which hung the sign "Old and Interesting" and begin scooping books willy-nilly into boxes, without even bothering to check what they were. One of the more successful of these, a hawk-nosed man in his forties who seemed to have gotten at least half the table into his box, shot off into a corner to examine his haul. With a rapid-fire motion he pulled each book out, inspected it front, back, and inside, and then either put it back carefully into his box or tossed it dismissively onto the floor.

As a result, we weren't there five seconds before we realized that this was not going to be the place where we found a book for $5 that would sell at auction for a quarter of a million. Even if there were such a book at this sale, so many dealers would be pummeling each other to get at it that the closest we would come to it would be the emergency room.

However, if you could ignore the jostling and the general rudeness, it really was a great sale. In the main auditorium we got a regular trade edition of *The Best and the Brightest* to replace our book-club edition, and first editions of the *The Battle Cry of Freedom,* James McPherson's Pulitzer Prize–winning history of the Civil War, and of *A Bright Shining Lie,* Neil Sheehan's brilliant study of John Paul Vann and America's folly in Vietnam. All were in first-rate condition. The penciled total for the three was $8, meaning we paid 16. In a used-book store, they would have been at least $60.

After about fifteen minutes, we wandered over to the literature tent, which in itself must have held close to half the sale. There we found, among other things, first editions of E. L. Doctorow's *Ragtime* and John O'Hara's *Assembly.*

By the end, we had filled up two decent-size shopping bags (supplied by the volunteers). Even at the doubled price, we spent less than $50.

We had paid for our purchases and were lugging our shopping bags across the lawn when we passed two men chatting. One was a short, rather corpulent man wearing a tight-fitting black T-shirt, black shorts, black socks, and once-white tennis sneakers. He was balding, had a ponytail, and was so pale that his skin looked like parchment.

The other, a man in his midthirties, wearing blue jeans and a HARD ROCK CAFE, LONDON T-shirt, said, THIS PLACE HAS REALLY GONE DOWNHILL.

The man in the black T-shirt flicked the remains of a cigarette into a half-filled plastic-foam cup of coffee that was sitting on the grass. In doing so, he tipped the cup over. Stale coffee and a number of decomposing cigarette butts spilled out onto the Pequot Library lawn.

"Yeah," he agreed, and with a rueful shake of his head, gathered up his shopping bags and walked away.

In addition to our haul, the sale had the considerable added advantage of introducing us to the library itself. For one thing, we discovered that there were two tall bookcases at the front of the library that had 1 and $2 books for sale all year round. Although the volunteers tried to hold out anything that was valuable and save it for the annual sale, every once in a while a first edition, something that would sell for 30 or $40 at a dealer's, would find its way to these bookcases. And, if you weren't hunting for anything collectible, but were simply looking for good reading copies, this was definitely the place to come. There were always biographies, commercial fiction, and seasonal books. Over the course of the following year, we stocked our entire collection of gardening and craft books for under $15.

Although we knew that there was a rare-book collection at the Pequot Library, it never occurred to us that it would be something in which we would be interested. Maybe it was the word "genealogy" that was always appended to "rare books," but we assumed that the collection would be local esoterica, minutes of old town meetings and such, so we never really asked about it.

But one night, about two months after the sale, we went to the grand opening reception of the new, larger Westport Barnes & Noble and met a man named Peter. We mentioned to him that we liked old books.

"I'm a book dealer," he said. He locked his eyes on us. He was a small, thin, intense man in his sixties. "What do you collect?"

"Well, we like—"

"I have a search service, too, if there's anything you want in particular."

"Well, not real—"

"Have you been to Pequot?"

"Wha—"

"It's a library in Southport. They have an excellent rare-book room."

"Oh, th—"

"I know the librarian there. I could give her a call and arrange for you to see the books."

"Well, th—"

"Or, better yet, I have something for you. If you're interested in rare books, you'll love our group. I'm a member of a rare-book discussion group. We meet once a month. Have you got an E-mail address?"

"Uh—"

"That's all right. I can send you a flyer."

Although we did not give him our address, shortly thereafter we discovered an envelope in our mailbox. Inside was the following notice *[sic]*:

Connecticut Rate & Fine Book Discussion Group
Meeting:
November 6—Pequot Library
All Meetings are scheduled on Thursdays and begin at
6:00 p.m.
Please join us and bring a friend.
All are welcome!
For further information, contact Nolan Lushington, Associate Professor, Department of Library Science and Instructional Technology.

There was a little note attached to this announcement with a paper clip. It read, *"You'll find this very interesting. Hope you can come, Peter."*

"Not a chance."

"Oh come on, Larry. It might be fun."

"Fun? A rare-book meeting? The people will be older than the books."

"Okay, so maybe *fun* is the wrong word. But it could be, well, interesting. There *will* be books there, you know. And tell the truth . . . aren't you curious to see what someone named Nolan Lushington looks like?"

"There is that."

"And the auditorium is big. We'll sit in the back. If it's boring, we can just slip out."

"I'll go on one condition. As soon as we walk in, I want to tell everyone that we have a baby-sitter and we have to leave by six-thirty."

"Six-thirty? That's only a half-hour."

"Okay, seven o'clock then."

"Don't you think that will look just a little obvious, Larry? Walking in and announcing that we have to leave in an hour?"

"I don't think subtlety will be required for this crowd. I'm not even sure everyone will be alive."

"Ha, ha. What if we tell everyone we have to leave and then it turns out to be fun?"

"That is a risk I am prepared to take."

When we arrived for the meeting, we saw immediately that we were not going to be able to slip out the back of the auditorium. That was because the meeting was not being held in the auditorium but rather at a large table in the main reading room. They could use the reading room because the regular library hours had ended. They could use the table because the group consisted of only seven people, including us. What was more, Nolan Lushington, we were told, could not make it.

Peter was there, however. He told everyone at the table how much he was enjoying reading *Used and Rare,* although he went out of his way to note that he had taken it out of the library rather than buying a copy.

While we waited for the meeting to begin, we went around the table and introduced ourselves. Directly across from us was a man named Lars. Lars appeared at first glance to be in his fifties, but after closer examination, might easily have been about thirty-five. He worked in some cloistered job at the post office or some such place, had light, thinning hair and pasty skin, and wore a short-sleeved button-down blue seersucker shirt. He was smiling and amiable but spoke in a kind of forced whisper. Lars glanced around a lot, doing so with quick jerky turns of his head. He was the kind of person whom Hollywood casts as the computer junkie who uses the Internet to lure young women to his apartment for deviate sex.

"We're Nancy and Larry Goldstone, and we have to leave no later than seven o'clock because we have a baby-sitter," we said.

At the far end of the table were two women, one of whom was

a children's librarian who was trying to move up the corporate ladder and work with the adult collection. She was extremely enthusiastic about the meeting although disappointed that "Nolan" was not going to be present. She said, "Nolan" in the same way that fourteen-year-old girls say, "Leonardo." The other woman was not a book person at all. When asked why she had come, she cocked her head to the right and said, "I'm with him."

"Hi," said the man next to her. He was about fifty, wearing a sport shirt and slacks. "I'm Richard Finchley. We came all the way from Danbury."

"Hi, Richard. Are you in the book trade?"

"Unfortunately not."

"What do you do then?"

"I'm an orthodontist."

Just two weeks before, our daughter's dentist had told us that she was most certainly going to need braces. As one, we turned up our smiles in Richard Finchley's direction.

Before we could inquire about the bibliophile discount, however, a woman pushed a rolling cart to the head of the table and turned to address the group.

"Hi!" she said. "I'm Danielle Carriera, and I'm the research librarian here at the Pequot Library. I'm so happy to be hosting tonight's rare-book discussion group. We'll be talking about the 'Art of the Book.' Welcome to Pequot!"

Danielle Carriera was not who we would have expected to be running the rare-book meeting. For one thing, she was only in her twenties, which made her about fifty years too young. She was dressed in a long skirt, sweater, and flowing scarf and was vivacious and attractive.

"Our library is one hundred years old, and the books you're going to see tonight have all been gifts," she continued. "They are part of our 'Art of the Book' collection here at Pequot."

She turned to the cart. There were books on each of its three shelves. It was difficult to tell what they were. One or two looked small, and there was one massive volume on the bottom.

"Let's start with the monks," she said decisively, withdrawing two books and placing them on the table. One of them was greatly oversize, and the other undersize. They looked like Mutt and Jeff.

"This is St. Gregory's letters from the twelfth century," Danielle said, opening the large one. It was bound in dirty white vellum on boards that were cracked and breaking. "It's an original twelfth-century illuminated manuscript of the French school. It's in Latin, with early French workmanship."

She opened the book, and there was the text, written in a beautiful spidery handwriting, the opening letter surrounded by an intricate design colored in sapphire blue, emerald green, red, and gold.

Everyone leaned closer to see.

"Why don't we pass it around the table?" Danielle suggested. "Here, you can start," and she passed the book to us.

We were startled. People don't offer you an eight-hundred-year-old book to play with every day. "You mean, we can turn the pages and everything? Don't we have to wear white gloves or something?"

Danielle smiled. "Just be careful," she said.

We bent over the manuscript. It was in incredibly good condition. Although we had seen individual leaves of illuminated manuscripts on display at the Morgan Library, those had been out of reach, in a cabinet under glass. Now we were touching something from the 1100s.

The paper was heavy. It felt rich and well made, like a linen wedding invitation, only not as stiff. "It's vellum," Danielle explained. "If you look closely, you can see the lines the monks drew to keep the writing even. And see these holes?" She pointed to spots on the paper that we had assumed had worn away over time. "Those were deliberately burned away. That's how they handled mistakes."

Danielle held up the second, smaller volume. "This next one is

St. Gregory's *Book of Hours,* also in Latin. We're not sure of the date, maybe fourteenth century." She turned to the first page. "Take a look at this," she said.

This time the illustrations surrounding the letters were even brighter, and they weren't simply designs as they were in the earlier manuscript. They were tiny pictures of people praying amid a swirl of royal blues, golds, reds, and greens.

There were some audible gasps here. Even the orthodontist's wife was impressed.

"You can see the texture in these colors, especially the gold," said Danielle. "Once again, you can see the lines they drew so that the letters would all be even. More than one person must have worked on these at the same time. If you look closely, you can see that the handwriting changes. Would you like me to pass this one around as well?"

Immediately, we delicately slid St. Gregory's letters over to the children's librarian and took possession of his *Book of Hours*. Paging through it, as before, you couldn't help but think of the monks six hundred years ago, bending carefully, suspended above these pages, agonizing over every letter. It seemed ironic that people who led such an otherwise grim, ascetic existence were capable of generating the creative energy that produced these works of great and lasting beauty.

"These look like musical notes," we said at one point.

"Yes," Danielle agreed. "We think perhaps it's a hymnal."

The next book Danielle produced looked older than the first two, although it wasn't. It had leather binding over wooden boards that was bubbled and cracked.

"This is an example of 'The Black Letter,'" Danielle announced. The printing was very small and the ink very black. "That's the name of the first printed type. This book was printed in 1487. You can see that the handwritten lines for evenness are gone. They didn't need them anymore because now they were printing.

"And here's a cookbook!" Danielle laughed, drawing a thin volume bound in pigskin from the cart. "It's called *The Platina,* and it was printed in Venice in 1475. It's much easier to read. The words are spaced out more, and there's more of a margin."

She handed this to us as well, and we flipped through the pages. Toward the back was the heading "CALAMARII." Italian cooking has apparently not changed all that much in five hundred years.

Then there was a 1502 Aldine Press book, "sort of the mass-market paperback of the sixteenth century," and an abridged gardener's dictionary from 1763 with intricate metal-plate engravings of people in a garden surrounded by fruit and shovels and cherubs. She even had Shakespeare First Folios, the first printing of a play, something we had never seen, only read about. This volume, which had been rebound, contained both *King Lear* and *Othello.*

And then, finally, Danielle reached to the bottom shelf of the cart and lifted out the huge clamshell case we'd noticed at the beginning. She laid it on the table and opened it.

"And this," she said, withdrawing a thick folio-size book with a blue cover, "is the Kelmscott Chaucer, possibly the most beautiful book ever to be printed. It's on blue paper boards with a linen spine. We have to be careful with this one, the gatherings are coming away. But on the inside, it's perfect." She opened the book to the title page. "This is William Morris's masterpiece," she said.

There is no equivalent for William Morris in today's society. Although he is principally remembered as a decorator whose wallpaper, fabric, and furniture designs are still popular, he also founded the Kelmscott Press, was a candidate for poet laureate, led the socialist party in Britain, and married a woman considered by many to be the most beautiful in England. You have to imagine Ralph Lauren being elected head of the UAW or Bill Clinton striding through the White House with bolts of red velvet under his arm to approximate William Morris's position in Victorian England.

He was born in 1834 to as soulless a pair of yuppies as any ever created by Tom Wolfe. His father, William Morris, Sr., made it big as a discount stockbroker in a London trading house. He died when his son was thirteen and left the family a fortune in speculative mining stocks. His mother, Emma, was a bourgeois consumer who liked big Georgian houses and four meals a day, plus snacks. According to Fiona MacCarthy's excellent biography, *William Morris: A Life for Our Time,* in discussing the origins of his love of beauty William Morris said that it "must have been inborn since neither his father or his mother nor any of his relations had the least idea of it."

He went to Oxford, where he struck up a friendship with an art student, Edward Burne-Jones, who was as poor as Morris was rich. After college they lived together in London, where Burne-Jones fell under the influence of another painter, Dante Gabriel Rossetti. Rossetti was a noted rake with a definite taste for the underside of London nightlife. With Burne-Jones at his heels, he hung out at studios, went to the theater, read and talked until the early hours of the morning, and honed his art in the decidedly un-Victorian manner of (among other things) sketching beautiful young women who needed the money. After experiencing this lifestyle vicariously for a while through Burne-Jones, Morris, who had been working long hours as an apprentice to an architect, abruptly switched to painting.

Morris threw himself into his new vocation with the intensity that was to become his trademark. Although his paintings were not especially good, he had fun with his buddies Burne-Jones and Rossetti—he loved hanging around with the boys—and met a lot of interesting people, one of whom was a stunning model, Janey Burden.

Janey was only eighteen, from a poor family, uneducated and lacking in culture and sophistication. What she had was height and hair—lots of it, dark and wild—and a kind of ethereal, withdrawn beauty. Rossetti had discovered Janey, but he had another girlfriend at the time, and, since models tended to be available whenever you needed them, he felt no great urgency about pursuing her. Morris, on the other hand, now twenty-three years old with a bang-up education in Latin and the classics but almost none in women, looked at Janey and saw Helen of Troy, Persephone, and Guinevere combined. He fell hopelessly in love and did something unthinkable, for which Rossetti was unprepared. He proposed.

Janey accepted. It would have been insanity not to, like a salesgirl at Bloomingdale's refusing John F. Kennedy, Jr. But she didn't love him, she loved Rossetti.

The marriage was a disaster.

Janey's adulterous relationships became infamous both for their openness and her propensity for choosing her husband's friends as her bedmates. Rossetti had eventually married also, but when his wife died soon after, Janey jumped in to take her place. She was so blatant about it that Morris, who by this time had started a design firm with Rossetti and Burne-Jones, bought a house in the country to at least get his wife and his partner out of London.

Not content with making Morris's life miserable when she wasn't with him, when she was with him, Janey moped. At some point early in her marriage, she gave up all attempts at the vertical and simply lay down on her couch. This was a source of great sexual fascination to everyone in Morris's circle, and they all painted her this way. Whenever a model was required, Janey was called in on her sofa. She's all over the sketches and paintings of the period, lying down and moping.

Why Morris tolerated his wife's behavior to the extreme degree that he did remains unclear, as were his reasons for staunchly remaining friends with her paramours. Perhaps it was the guilt he felt about his bourgeois upbringing, his trust fund, his girth, and his self-perceived lack of sexual finesse. Also, he loved her.

As his outlet, Morris threw a staggering amount of energy into his work, which at the time was decorating rich people's houses. Although there was a history of craftsmanship in England dating to the Middle Ages, interior design was (as it still is) considered one of "the minor arts." Morris took it up a peg on both the artistic and social ladders. The firm, Morris & Co. (he put up the money), became all the rage in London in the 1860s. In addition to layouts, Morris & Co. designed much of what it placed in its clients' homes.

Morris may have been acquiescent where Janey was concerned, but he bowled over everyone else. In the 1950s, Max Beerbohm satirized Morris's personality and approach to his clients in a radio broadcast entitled "Hethway Speaking" (actually, in this case, it's Morris speaking), which was quoted in Fiona MacCarthy's biography:

> "We'll let you have everything at two per cent above cost of production, by Jiminy, because we're blooming beginners and you're our friend. Hooray! I've got *all* the designs in my head now . . . I see your whole blessed room for you, all clear before me. You shall have a great cedar chair—*there,* in the middle—like Odin's throne; and a settle—all along *this* wall—to seat a regiment. And Ned Burne-Jones will do the stained glass for your window—Life of La Belle Iseult; and Ford Madox Brown shall do the panels of the settle—Boyhood of Chaucer; and"—he strode up and down brandishing his arms—"there's a young chap named William De Morgan who'll do the tiles for the hearth; and my wife shall embroider the edges of the window-curtains—you know that green serge we've got, Faulkner—glorious. And by Jove we'll"—but here he slipped and sat with a terrific crash on the parquet. "That's just what I was going to speak about," he continued, sitting; "this isn't a floor, it's a sheet of ice: it won't do; we must have good honest rough oaken boards with bulrushes," he cried, bounding to his feet, "—strewn bulrushes. And we'll have a—"
>
> "One moment, Morris," I begged. "When you say *we,*

do you mean simply yourself and Faulkner and the Company, or do you include *me*?"

"But of course I include you," he said. "Why, hang it all, the *room's* yours."

"That's just what I was beginning to doubt," I said.

Wallpaper and furniture were just the beginning. From there he moved to looming and tapestry, dyes and woodstuffs, and wrote poetry. He eventually produced a four-part series modeled after Chaucer's *Canterbury Tales,* called *The Earthly Paradise. The Earthly Paradise* was a huge popular success and made Morris something of a cult figure. It was after Tennyson's death in 1892 that he was considered for poet laureate. Aware that his politics would prevent his being chosen, he withdrew his name from the list of active candidates.

Barbara Tuchman, one of our favorite historians, wrote about this same poet laureate appointment in *The Proud Tower: A Portrait of the World Before the War: 1890 –1914.* Since Gladstone, the prime minister at the time, also considered Swinburne an immoral degenerate and thus as unsuitable as Morris, the field was left open to lesser players:

> All other candidates were mediocrities, one of whom, Sir Lewis Morris [no relation to William], offered an opening to what a contemporary called "the most spontaneously witty thing ever uttered in England." Morris, author of an effusion entitled *The Epic of Hades,* who wanted the Laureateship badly, complained to Oscar Wilde in the days before his ruin, "There is a conspiracy of silence against me, a conspiracy of silence. What ought I to do, Oscar?" "Join it," replied Wilde.*

*Barbara W. Tuchman, *The Proud Tower: a Portrait of the World Before the War: 1890 –1914,* 1966, New York: The Macmillan Company, p. 34.

Somewhere along the line, Morris became a socialist, and he took politics as seriously as he took everything else. He marched, he rallied, he attended meetings, he served on committees, he lectured, and he even got himself arrested for disturbing the peace. In his own affairs, however, socialist principles seem to have gotten lost. Morris presided like a lord over every economic enterprise in which he participated. He had weavers and loomers and dyers and quilters and tapestry-makers working for him, and his labor force not only failed to share in the profits of their work, they couldn't make the simplest decision without him. He told them what time to get to work, what to do at work, when to take a break, and when not to take a break. His attitude toward his various enterprises was summed up nicely by his daughter May, when she recounted the conversation that he had with his friend and neighbor Emery Walker on the day he proposed establishing the Kelmscott Press: "Will you go into partnership with me? . . . But mind I shall want to do everything my own way."

And that was just what he did. In 1890, near the end of his remarkable life (he died in 1896 at the age of sixty-two), William Morris took the sum total of his experience, his craftsmanship, his love of beauty, his love of nature, his love of art, his love of wallpaper, and his love of old books (he had possibly the best private library of fifteenth-century manuscripts in England), as well as the loves and experiences and talents of all of his best friends, and poured it into the making of fine books.

Morris didn't just design these books. As with everything else with which he became involved, he immersed himself in every detail of their manufacture. The result was the Kelmscott Press (named after the house in which he lived), which produced just over fifty books in seven years, the most famous of which is the Chaucer.

One of the reasons he gave for starting the press was his distress over modern printing. England was going through the Industrial Revolution, and Morris hated it. He hated the new buildings, he despised the new factories, and most of all, he *loathed* the new type. It gave him a headache to read the printing in a modern book, it was so ugly, he said. And the illustrations weren't any better. So, since *his* ideal literature took the form of a medieval manuscript, he attempted, not to copy the font exactly, but to interpret it for a nineteenth-century audience. To do this, he had to invent his own type, which he did by sitting down at a desk in his workroom and painstakingly copying the letters of fourteenth- and fifteenth-century books over and over again, for hours at a time, until he was satisfied that he knew the style well enough to create his own.

He created three new fonts. The first was called the Golden Type, the second the Troy Type, and the last font, the one he used in the Chaucer, the Chaucer Type. In *The Kelmscott Press: A History of William Morris's Typographical Adventure,* by William S. Peterson, there are reproductions of some of Morris's notes that survive from this period. They consist primarily of pieces of paper on which are drawn a single letter of the alphabet over and over again with minute changes in each attempt, the whole surrounded by scribbled notes. For example, on the "h" paper, Morris wrote: *"a tendency to make everything a little too rigid & square is noticeable: Can this be remedied."*

And of course he had to have his own paper made to his own precise specifications, and he had to have Edward Burne-Jones, who was by this time a baronet, create the woodcuts, some of which used Janey as the model, and then the borders had to be designed by hand and the ink made to be just brilliant enough, and the whole bound in exactly the right kind of pigskin or linen, depending upon which version of the book was being ordered, and so on and so on, so that, when a Kelmscott book is finally placed in front of you, as it was placed in front of us at the rare-book meeting at the Pequot Library, the whole of it is so infused with the spirit of a man born more than 150 years ago that you can actually hear the work bellow—THIS IS ME!!

"Here's my favorite page," said Danielle, turning to an illustration of the tale "Romaunt of the Rose." It featured a number of women dressed in long, flowing empire-waisted dresses, dancing in a bacchanalian manner, two of them kissing. Surrounding the illustration and the type set underneath was a border of curling leaves and vines. "Look at the detail in the woodcut—the dresses look like they have weight to them. Edward Burne-Jones was famous for his ability to draw and paint fabric. You feel the folds in his draperies.

"Despite its size and the fact that it is printed in old English, William Morris meant this book to be read," Danielle continued. "You see, he studied everything that we looked at here tonight—the twelfth- and fourteenth-century manuscripts, the Black Letter print, Shakespeare, and the Aldine Press, all in his attempt to create a book that people would want to hold *and* read, not a coffee-table book, but a decorated book. And the result is really something special, I think."

She started turning the pages so we could see. The paper was like the paper in the illustrated manuscripts, heavy and tactile. The ink was very black against the paper. It was double columned with margin notes in red.

"I can't let you handle this one," said Danielle, "but if you tell me what you want to look at, I'll turn the pages for you."

We were just about to ask her if we could see "The Wife of Bath" when Peter interrupted.

"Why don't you bring it over here," he said. "They have to go."

"Huh?"

"It's seven o'clock." He tapped the face of his watch. "They have a baby-sitter," he explained.

Chapter 3

The road to which the name of Kevin Rita's shop, On The Road Books, referred was Route 44, which runs northwest to southeast in northern Connecticut. The shop itself was in Canton, about halfway between Torrington and Hartford. After Mariab, we had been so determined to see the rest of Kevin's books that we had even been willing to drive through Torrington in order to do so. Torrington is a grim, depressed town, made worse by the fact that the traffic lights are set in such a way that, no matter how fast you drive, each one turns red just before you get to it, then stays red for what seems like ten minutes, thus providing the opportunity to appreciate the grimness and depressedness of Torrington for that much longer.

Canton, about ten miles east, is hardly a town at all, just a series of retail outlets and mini-malls set on both sides of Route 44. On the Road Books was in a small clapboard house that used to hold both the general store and the post office. In addition to the bookshop, the occupants of the building included a hardwood flooring company, a BMW motorcycle sales and service outlet, and Elegant Touch, a nail salon.

We walked in the front door and saw Kevin squeezed behind a small desk set in a tiny cubicle in the front. He was surrounded by knocked-together, closely packed, floor-to-ceiling bookcases, standard decor for used-book shops where stock had overwhelmed available space. As we walked over to say hello, we almost stepped on a large, inert, brown and black furry object that turned out to be a dog.

"That's Snagsby," said Kevin.

"Snagsby?"

"From *Bleak House.* You know, Snagsby & Snagsby, the barristers. I named him that because he looked like an Edwardian barrister."

"What kind?" we asked. "Of dog, not lawyer."

Kevin puffed up visibly. "An Airedale. The king of the terriers," he proclaimed.

Many shop owners might have hesitated before allowing a dog, especially a large hunting dog, to be in such close proximity to rare books, but Snagsby, it turned out, was perfectly suited to his environment. Snagsby was mellow. So mellow, in fact, that it was often necessary to browse for some period of time before having the opportunity to observe Snagsby moving, with great deliberation, from one place to sleep to another. In addition, Snagsby seemed to have mastered the trick of sleeping without appearing to be breathing.

"Do you know what people ask me sometimes?" asked Kevin with great umbrage. Snagsby was, at that moment—and for some number of previous moments—sleeping with his back against one of the bookcases. "They ask, 'Is that a real dog?' I think, you *nitwit,* what are the alternatives? It's either a *real* dog, a *dead* dog, or a *stuffed* dog. Now which of those do you think it probably is?"

We nodded sympathetically. We avoided mentioning that the same question had occurred to us. Anyone who would name a dog after a character in *Bleak House* was clearly our kind of guy.

"I'm an Anglophile," Kevin added. "Being Irish and Italian, it's kind of a tough act to pull off, but I do my best."

The front room contained a nice selection of general used books, some sets, and better-than-average-quality paperbacks. As with most used-book stores, the stock was divided by category, reflecting the owner's interests. Here, for example, there was an excellent selection of books about South Africa, and literary biographies, in addition to a small but choice section on American history and another on poetry. The books in the fiction section were well-priced hardcovers and in very good condition. The selection was good but not extraordinary. There were some interesting things in the literature section, books that we had not seen very often, like *How Green Was My Valley* by Richard Llewellyn, but none of the exquisite, meticulously chosen works of fiction that Kevin had brought to Mariab.

"I think you'll be more interested in the next room," he said, gesturing toward an archway just to the left of the desk.

When we walked through, it was like being in a different and substantially more upscale shop. Where the first room was purely functional, the middle room had been set up to be aesthetic, and by someone who knew how to do it. Floor-to-ceiling bookcases lined the walls, but these were carefully constructed and finished, and there were no free-standing bookcases in the center to cut off the room. Instead, there was a large library table neatly stacked with books, eclectic in subject but creating a striking visual effect. There were books on gardening with green covers highlighting jumbles of delicate pink roses; cookbooks with brightly colored dust jackets; books about places like Provence and Tuscany; art books; unusual books about the Victorian Age; and a smattering of foreign first editions and some more poetry. Original, framed photographs of Raymond Carver, James Salter, and Isaac Babel were hung on pillars in the center of the room. With the open floor plan and crisp lighting, the space seemed like a hybrid of a bookshop and an art gallery.

Modern firsts took up the entire wall to the left of the doorway. There was a lot of literary fiction and a number of U.K. firsts of American fiction, as we had seen at Mariab. Most were in excellent condition, and almost nothing was over one hundred dollars. There was also a section devoted to British firsts (of British titles), one for women's fiction, more literary biography, some Asian firsts, and an extensive area devoted to gastronomy.

"I love cooking, too," noted Kevin.

We picked out a first U.K. of *The Last Hurrah* by Edwin O'Connor, with a distinctive black, gray, and steel blue dust jacket showing a tousled-haired Irishman standing in front of a gaggle of microphones; *Dos Passos: A Life* by Virginia Spencer Carr; and a beautiful, bright-as-new copy of the 1986 Random House edition of *Ulysses* with the corrected text.

We saw an archway leading into a third room.

"That's Janice's gallery." Kevin's wife, Janice La Motta, was a painter who ran the Paessegio Art Gallery as an adjunct to but separately from the bookshop.

"*Paessegio* means countryside or landscape in Italian," said Kevin, "but it also means passage, which is kind of what we try to do . . . take you to another place."

We walked through the archway. Janice was exhibiting an award-winning Irish artist, a Catholic from Ulster who was now living in Brooklyn. Her work was mostly collages of bare trees and outdoor scenes overlaid on extracts of political tracts. They were unusual and exceedingly well done, with a bleak, November feeling. We looked around the room again, at the stark white walls and minimalist layout. It was as if the twister from *The Wizard of Oz* had honed in on Manhattan, struck Soho, lifted a gallery, and dropped it on Route 44 in Canton.

"Do you get a lot of people here?" We didn't know quite how else to ask the question. Maybe Kevin didn't know that his location might be considered by some as inconvenient.

"Oh, yes," Kevin replied. "A surprising number. Janice has a great eye. The gallery is written up all the time."

"Still," we persisted, "wouldn't it be better if you were in some spot that's . . . easier to get to?"

"Sure," Kevin said. "We've thought about moving to Hartford. But it's hard to find just the right space."

On our way back to the desk to pay for our books, we made one last pass through the modern-firsts section in the middle room. We noticed a copy of *The Haunting of Hill House* by Shirley Jackson, which we had missed the first time. The book had a gray, not especially arresting dust jacket and was in okay, but not great, condition. *The Haunting of Hill House* had been made into a wonderfully creepy movie called *The Haunting* with Julie Harris and Claire Bloom. We'd heard that the book was good too, so we checked the price. Seventy-five dollars.

It was only because of our profligacy after Mariab, when we had kept both editions of *Mrs. Bridge,* that we didn't yet again say, "Oh, why not," and just chuck *The Haunting of Hill House* on the top of the pile. Instead, in a rare if not unique exercise of self-discipline, we put it back on the shelf, then stood and looked at it, congratulating ourselves on our virtue. We did tell ourselves, however, that if the book was still there the next time we came to Canton, it would be fate, and we would buy it.

Two months later, we walked through the door of On the Road Books, hardly stopped to say hello, and made right for the middle room and the first-edition section. *The Haunting of Hill House* was no longer on the shelf.

"Sold it, huh?"

"Ten minutes ago," said Kevin. He took us back to the front room and introduced us to a high-priced out-of-state dealer in modern firsts whose catalog we regularly received. *The Haunting of Hill House* was sitting on the top of a stack of books on Kevin's desk. We wondered for a moment what would happen if we grabbed it and said, "You can't have that! It's ours!"

Instead, we meekly shook hands with the dealer and shrugged. "Fortunes of war," we said, smiling with complete insincerity.

So much for virtue.

(Furious at having blown it, we kept wondering what the dealer would charge for a book for which he paid, after the 20-percent dealer discount and no tax, sixty-dollars. When we got his catalog about a month later, we found out.

> JACKSON, Shirley. THE HAUNTING OF HILL HOUSE. NY: Viking 1959.
>
> A couple of tiny puncture marks on the rear board, a little soiling to the cloth portion of the binding, a very good copy in a very good dustwrapper with some of the usual rubbing at the extremities and a little soiling and a tiny puncture on the rear panel. Basis for the film *The Haunting*. The first edition of this modern horror classic is increasingly scarce.
>
> $500

"Oh no," the dealer told Kevin, when he found out we knew. "They're going to make me look like a price gouger."

We would never do something like that. We're not bad losers.)

After the dealer left, our friend Jocelyn came in. Jocelyn was the book editor at the *Hartford Courant*. We had met her when she came to our house to interview us for an article on *Used and Rare*. Usually after an interview, you never see the person again, but Jocelyn was witty, and intelligent and loved books—not someone to abandon lightly just because she wrote (accurately) that one of us talks all the time. We thought she would like On The Road, which was much closer to her than it was to us, so we asked if she wanted to meet us there and then have lunch later.

Jocelyn has short dark hair, granny glasses that she cleans every now and then with the sort of detached absorption adopted by actors playing district atotorneys, and a serious, studious manner. We introduced her to Kevin.

"Are you interested in anything in particular?" he asked her.

Jocelyn paused. Until you get to know her well, Jocelyn seems to weigh her words carefully. "I'm not really a collector," she said finally, "but I am a fan of Bloomsbury."

If she had uttered the words "I just bought the winning Powerball ticket, and I'm handing it over to you," Kevin could not have brightened more visibly.

"Really," he said. "So am I. Tell me," he said, leaning forward conspiratorially, "have you read *Deceived with Kindness*?"

"You mean, the one Angelica wrote about her marriage to Bunny and how it destroyed her life? Yes, I saw that one. Did you read Vita's letters to Victoria? So sensual."

"Of course. They're classic. You know, there's a biography of Duncan in the works."

"Who's doing it?"

"Frances Spalding. Same woman who did Vanessa."

Jocelyn frowned. "I haven't seen that one."

"I think I have it," said Kevin and strode over to a bookshelf, with Jocelyn right behind.

We blinked at each other and trotted after them. Up until then, Bloomsbury had meant to us Virginia Woolf and some other characters of whom we were vaguely aware who had just been incorporated in a not very good film called *Carrington* with Jonathan Pryce and Emma Thompson. The sum total of our Bloomsbury collection was cheap reading copies of *Mrs. Dalloway* and *To the Lighthouse.*

Kevin was handing a book over to Jocelyn. "You might like this one," he said.

Jocelyn squinted at the book and then at the shelf from which it had come. "You have a very nice selection here," she said. "Oh, *Ottoline,"* she almost cooed, reaching up to the shelf.

We had never heard Jocelyn coo before. Jocelyn was not a cooer.

"Who is Ottoline?" we asked.

"Ottoline Morrell," said Jocelyn. "She was kind of this larger-than-life society woman. She had a fling with Roger."

"Who's Roger?" We were a little puzzled by all this first-name stuff. The only other people we had ever heard talk like this were the local nannies discussing *Days of Our Lives* and Chicago Bulls fans talking about Michael and Scottie.

"Roger Fry. You know, Vanessa's lover."

"Who's—"

"I'll tell you what I like about Bloomsbury," Kevin broke in. "I really like its existence as a cultural and historical milieu, a self-nurturing set of intellectuals somewhat at odds with the public morality. What makes Bloomsbury greater than the sum of its parts was the pervasive, overwhelming . . ." he sighed longingly, "*sexuality.* Nothing we read today in the tabloids is anywhere near as shocking as the intersecting lines of Bloomsbury."

Oh. We stared up at the shelves of books.

"Well, if you were going to read about Bloomsbury, where would be a good place to start?" we asked.

Kevin and Jocelyn considered.

"Well," said Jocelyn slowly, "the Quentin Bell biography is interesting." She looked at Kevin for confirmation.

Kevin nodded. "Got it right here," he said, reaching up. "A nice copy, too."

He handed us *Virginia Woolf: A Biography* by Quentin Bell. "Quentin Bell was Vanessa's son," he said.

"Who's Vanessa?"

"Vanessa Bell was Virginia Woolf's sister. She was an artist. I'm kind of half in love with Vanessa," said Kevin.

"Is she still alive?"

"Oh no, she's dead."

The cover of the Bell biography had a photo of a young Virginia Woolf in half-profile, staring off into the distance. She had a low forehead, a remarkably long face, and a prominent chin. She would in no way by contemporary standards be considered pretty. Yet there was something about her that was utterly arresting and intensely sexual.

"It's got a nice bookplate by Rockwell Kent on the front endpaper," Kevin pointed out. "The previous owner was a friend of his."

Oh, well, that made all the difference.

"Okay, we'll take it," we said.

"This is probably going to be the last time you come here," Kevin said as he was totaling up our purchases.

"Why?"

"I'm opening a new store in West Hartford," he said proudly. "We found a great space."

"You're closing this one?"

"No, I'm keeping this one, but I'm going to keep it pretty much a straight used-book store. The one in West Hartford is going to be just like the middle room, only larger. It's such a great space. I'm going to personally pick every book that goes in there. Everything in that shop is going to be there because it means something to me. There are books that I know I could sell that aren't going to be there. There's nothing wrong with them, but they're just not special."

"What about the gallery?"

"Oh, that's coming, too."

"Congratulations. How did you find the space?"

"The guy who used to rent it is retiring."

"Was he a book dealer?"

"Oh, no," said Kevin.

"What kind of business did he have?"

"A kennel," said Kevin. He handed us our books. "You'd better be careful if you start collecting Bloomsbury," he said. "You're going to need some more bookcases. There's a lot of it."

One of the reasons that there is so much Bloomsbury is the sheer number of participants and their collective long-windedness. The core group—although even this is in dispute—seems to have consisted of: Virginia and Leonard Woolf, Vanessa and Clive Bell, Lytton Strachey, Roger Fry, Duncan Grant, and John Maynard Keynes. However, flitting in and out of this assemblage were also Dora Carrington, T. S. Eliot, E. M. Forster, Vita Sackville-West, Ottoline Morrell, and any number of others. Everybody painted or wrote: they produced oils, watercolors, sketches, decorative panels, painted furniture, dust jackets, novels, biographies, short stories, reviews, literary criticism, memoirs, diaries, and, finally, letters. Letters and letters and letters. There weren't any telephones in those days, at least not in the beginning. If you wanted to communicate with someone, you either went to see them or you wrote. These people wrote. And because they were all distinguished people (or intended to be), they wrote for posterity. Virginia Woolf alone, in addition to all of her other work, left something on the order of thirty-five hundred letters.

Then there were all the people who came after Bloomsbury, Vanessa's children and their relatives, and *they* wrote; they wrote memoirs and biographies of all their parents' friends, and, of course, being related, they came under criticism for being prejudiced, so academically credentialed people had to step in and redo all the biographies, and it turned out to be such a good business that today if you want to read about Bloomsbury, you've got something on the order of twenty-five nine-hundred-page biographies to choose from.

But for all of the prodigious intellectual output, the continued fascination with Bloomsbury boils down to the fact that the history of their relationships is enough to successfully plot several daytime soap operas. To be as concise as possible, and necessarily not incorporating all the facets and detours of everyone's relationships, the principal story line goes something like this:

The Stephens were a large Victorian family living in England in the late 1800s. The father, Leslie, was a man of letters. He wrote several literary biographies and was the editor of *The Dictionary of National Biography,* a gargantuan enterprise, that would eventually result in sixty-three volumes encompassing the lives of 29,120 people. There was a lot of proofreading involved, which he hated, and this made him grouchy. Also, his first wife died, leaving him with only one child, Laura, who unfortunately was either retarded or insane or both. His new wife, Julia, was beautiful but sorrowful, having lost *her* first husband at the tender age of twenty-four. Julia had a mother who wrote the following sort of missives to her nearly every day: "My own Heart, She says it is impossible that Gruyere cheese should have remained two years in the bowels." Julia also had three children by her first marriage: George, Stella, and Gerald.

Julia and Leslie had four children of their own: Vanessa, beautiful and artistic; Thoby, tall, handsome, and brilliant; Virginia, beautiful and brooding; and Adrian, the younger brother, who hung around and in later life did things like dress himself up in blackface and turban as the emperor of Abyssinia mumbling things like "Bunga-Bunga" in order to trick the British Navy (successfully, by the way) into showing him and some of his friends (including Virginia, who was dressed as "Prince Mendax," a derivative of the word *liar* in Latin) around their latest warship.

Adored mother Julia died when Virginia was twelve, leaving her with her first bout of madness. Father never recovered from the sorrow and leaned heavily on Stella (Julia's daughter by her first marriage). Stella was in love with Jack Hills, a young solicitor. Jack asked Stella to marry him, but she refused because of Leslie's disapproval. Meanwhile, Virginia and Vanessa fell victim to sexual harassment by stepbrother George; no penetration, apparently, but still enough to be distasteful; also, he forced them to go to parties. Jack asked Stella to marry him again. Stella refused, again because of Leslie. Some indication that Leslie was falling in love with Stella. Jack asked a third time, Stella gave in to true love, Leslie gnashed his teeth, and Stella and Jack got married and went away on a romantic foreign honeymoon, during which Stella contracted some weird illness, and died three months later. Everybody mourned for about a year, whereupon Jack fell in love with Vanessa. Unfortunately it was against the law at the time to marry your dead sister's husband, and, besides, the rest of the family was shocked, so nothing much came of it.

Meanwhile, Thoby had hotfooted it out to Cambridge, where he was inducted into the number-one secret society, the Apostles. There he met, and engaged in long, penetrating, impassioned discussions on Homer, art, and the meaning of life and sex with such future luminaries and Bloomsbury members as Lytton Strachey, Desmond MacCarthy, Clive Bell, Saxon Sydney-Turner, and, later, Duncan Grant and Leonard Woolf. Thoby graduated just about the time that his father, old Leslie Stephen, who had become even more crotchety and unpleasant in old age, particularly to Vanessa, who had to keep the household accounts, had the good grace to die and leave his children a sizable fortune.

It can be argued that this generous action on the part of Leslie Stephen—that is to say, dying while his children were all in their early twenties or late teens and leaving them bereft of parental intervention but otherwise comfortably well-off—more than any other single factor is responsible for the cult of Bloomsbury, which still exists today, almost a century later. Because what the four Stephen children—all of them securely upper-class, highly intelligent, and superbly educated—did afterward was to dump the gloomy family mansion in the respectable part of town, lease themselves a new house in Bloomsbury, an area approved of by none of their remaining relatives but by all of their twenty-something friends, and proceed to have themselves a rip-roaring good time.

Vanessa painted, Virginia wrote, and Thoby brought all of his friends over every Thursday evening after dinner for enlightening conversation. It was during this period that the Bloomsbury reputation of sleeping with whosoever happened to be available at the moment, male or female, was securely established. Over the course of the next fifteen years, the following group members all coupled (and uncoupled) with each other: Lytton Strachey with John Maynard Keynes, Lytton Strachey with Duncan Grant, Lytton Strachey with Dora Carrington; Vanessa with Clive Bell, Vanessa with John

Maynard Keynes, Vanessa with Roger Fry, Vanessa with Duncan Grant; John Maynard Keynes with Duncan Grant, John Maynard Keynes with a little Russian ballerina named Lydia Lopokova, whom he eventually married; Adrian Stephen with Duncan Grant; Duncan Grant with David "Bunny" Garnett; Virginia Stephen with Clive Bell (chastely), Virginia Stephen with Leonard Woolf, Virginia Woolf with Vita Sackville-West. There's more, but this gives a nice flavor for the general group ethos, which can be summed up by the sort of incisive comment the group and Lytton Strachey in particular were known for. Upon arriving at Clive and Vanessa Bell's apartment one evening, Lytton noticed a stain on Vanessa's dress. "Semen?" he inquired.

Of course, there was more soap opera to come: In the fall of 1906 the Stephen children decided to take a holiday in Greece. You would think they would have learned from their stepsister Stella's experience, but no, they went, and Vanessa got so sick that it took her and Virginia a while to get back to England. Thoby went on ahead, and when the sisters got back, they found *him* sick. Clive Bell came to take care of all of them; Vanessa got better, but Thoby died. He was twenty-six. Clive Bell waited two days and then asked Vanessa to marry him (she had refused him at least twice before); this time she said yes.

Vanessa and Clive got married, and Virginia went to keep house with Adrian. Vanessa got pregnant, had her first child, Julian, and became absorbed in motherhood. Clive felt neglected, so, looking around for something to do, he decided to fall in love with Virginia. Virginia reciprocated his feelings, although it is unclear whether the relationship was actually consummated. Possibly her husband's and sister's fooling around behind her back had something to do with Vanessa's publicly dancing topless and then having sex with John Maynard Keynes and after that getting involved with Roger Fry, an artist taken with the Postimpressionist movement in France. Roger was older and married to a woman residing in a lunatic asylum.

Virginia got tired of Clive, or Clive got tired of her; it's difficult to tell which. Also, she was having more and more trouble with her madness—she produced her first novel, *The Voyage Out,* and had a breakdown over the reviews—so the Bloomsbury group looked around for someone to marry her. This was trickier than it looked, for although Virginia was considered beautiful, she also had a habit of ranting incoherently and trying to throw herself out of windows. (She did have a number of unsuitable candidates. Lytton Strachey, a notorious homosexual, once proposed to her, and to his chagrin she said yes, so he had to call it off the next day. He wrote to his brother James: "In my efforts to escape, I had a decided reverse the other day . . . I proposed to Virginia, and was accepted. It was an awkward moment, as you may imagine, especially as I realised, the very minute it was happening, that the whole thing was repulsive to me.")

The group came up with Leonard Woolf, just back from a stint with the British Foreign Office in Ceylon. Leonard was perfect. He was the right age, he was already a member of the group, he had idolized Virginia since he'd first set eyes on her when she visited Thoby at Cambridge, he had no real conception of her illness, and he was Jewish. Not even upper-class Jewish; only solidly middle-class Jewish—an extraordinary alliance for someone of Virginia Stephen's rarefied British background. What no one in the family bothered to clarify for Leonard was that Virginia was *only* available to him because she *was* crazy and the family needed someone who could comfortably be imposed upon. A man of Lytton Strachey's aristocratic background would most certainly have confined her, after much public soul-searching, to an insane asylum, as did Roger Fry his wife and T. S. Eliot his.

Leonard nonetheless leaped at his chance. He was so infatuated with Virginia and the world she represented it is likely that even if the case had been made plain to him he would have proposed anyway. After stalling around a bit, Virginia eventually did what everyone wanted and accepted Leonard. Vanessa, upon whose shoulders the burdens of Virginia's madness had seemed destined to fall, breathed a big sigh of relief. The bridegroom spent the rest of his life making sure Virginia got to bed at a decent hour and recording every single moment and mood of her day in his diary in an effort to anticipate the course of her illness.

There were more exploits over time, of course. Adrian fell in love with a predominently but not exclusively homosexual artist, Duncan Grant, whom Vanessa deliberately took away when she got tired of Roger Fry. Vanessa conceived her third child, Angelica, on one of the rare occasions when Duncan actually slept with her, and then she passed her off as Clive's daughter so effectively that when Angelica grew up she married Bunny Garnett, one of Duncan's lovers, which didn't do much for her psyche but gave her a terrific topic for a memoir. Virginia found sex with Leonard unsatisfying and made the mistake of telling Vanessa, who promptly broadcasted the information that Virginia was frigid to the rest of the group so that the Woolfs' sexual troubles came under general scrutiny; this of course did nothing to help the situation, so what little she and Leonard shared, shall we say, petered out altogether and Virginia reputedly fell instead into a lesbian affair with Vita Sackville-West.

Although it is often difficult to separate the quality of the work the members of the Bloomsbury group produced from the aura with which the group surrounded itself, there was some undeniable talent at play there. John Maynard Keynes, who when last seen was boffing Vanessa on a couch in full view of a roomful of people, became the preeminent economist of his time and philosophic godfather of the New Deal. E. M. Forster, whose works include *A Passage To India, A Room with a View,* and *Howard's End,* is still considered one of the finest novelists of his generation. T. S. Eliot's literary reputation remains undiminished.

As for the core group, a Vanessa Bell painting goes for thousands, a Duncan Grant for more, and works by both are part of the permanent collections of prestigious museums. Lytton Strachey, although not quite achieving the literary notoriety of some of the others, is nonetheless still praised for *Eminent Victorians,* an irreverent group biography, and his personality and one-liners still, more than anyone else's personify the combination of wit and sex that is the essence of Bloomsbury's appeal.

And then there was Virginia. Crazy Virginia, who eventually killed herself by throwing herself into the river behind her house, because she felt she was going mad again. ("I begin to hear voices, and can't concentrate," she wrote in her suicide note to Leonard.) Virginia surpassed them all. She alone in the group became, and remains, a transcendent figure. Although she has today been adopted as a feminist icon, she was in fact apolitical during her lifetime and focused completely on her fiction. And it was an offshoot of this consuming passion that has provided Bloomsbury with perhaps its most enduring legacy.

It began as something of a lark. Virginia and Leonard had often talked about starting a private press, but it had remained just talk until one day when they happened by a small printing-supply shop and saw a handpress through the window. On a whim, they walked in and bought it. Since they'd had no formal (or informal) training in printing, and knew no one who printed, and in fact had no idea how the machine even worked, they took the precaution of including a how-to book in their purchase. Suitably armed, they went home and started the Hogarth Press, named after the house they happened to be living in.

If the Kelmscott Press was the product of years and years of training and experience and attention to detail, the Hogarth Press was the product of tenacious ineptitude. In the beginning, Virginia laid the type and mixed up the *h*'s and the *n*'s. They couldn't get the ink right, they couldn't get the woodcuts right, they had no idea about paper, they couldn't get anyone to help them out, and they spent hours and hours in their basement covered in ink. Then, when a sheet finally did make it off the press, they forgot to proofread it. It is ironic that today the early volumes in particular are even more valuable to collectors precisely because Virginia and Leonard's technique was such that much of what they produced has not held up as well as books centuries older.

Their first book was *Two Stories,* one by Virginia and one by Leonard. The book featured woodcut illustrations by Dora Carrington, which so upset Vanessa that, after *Two Stories,* she did all the artwork for the press herself. The book came out in July 1917 and sold out the entire run of 134 copies, netting a profit of seven pounds.

Thrilled because they had made a profit, regardless of how small, the Woolfs threw themselves into printing with renewed energy. They published their own work and those of their friends. And because their friends happened to include E. M. Forster and T. S. Eliot, their press became important completely out of proportion to the professionalism with which they ran it. (For example, they turned down *Ulysses* because it was so long they couldn't face the work involved in typesetting it—all those *n*'s and *h*'s—although there also is some indication that Virginia was envious of Joyce's artistry.)

Virginia published *Kew Gardens, To the Lighthouse, Jacob's Room, A Room of One's Own, The Years,* and *Between the Acts* (posthumously), among others, through the Hogarth Press. Over time they got better at bookmaking, and because they always used the same artist, the books had a distinctive style. They were simple and unpretentious, stylish but comfortable, the physical representation of the Bloomsbury ideal of bringing art into daily life and particularly into domestic arrangements.

And so, if there is a way, today, to hold a piece of Bloomsbury in your hand, it is by picking up a Hogarth Press book.

Kevin opened his new shop in December 1997, and he was right—we haven't been back to Canton since. He had a lot of trouble choosing a name. He finally settled on Brick Walk Book Shop because there's a brick sidewalk at the back of the store.

Brick Walk quickly became an oasis for us. Every two months

or so, whenever we got too tired or bored or crabby or depressed, we got in the car and took the hour-or-so drive to West Hartford. As Kevin had promised, the Brick Walk Book Shop was just like the middle room at On The Road, only more so. The ceilings were high, the walls white, and plate-glass windows at either end let in a lot of light, so the place felt spacious and airy. Janice's gallery occupied the first third of the shop and set the mood immediately when you walked in.

The books were in the middle and back. Beautiful old oak glass-fronted bookcases lined the wall on the left. ("Aren't they great?" Kevin exulted. "They came from the old Bond Hotel in Hartford. Believe it or not, they came with the store. I don't know what the other guy kept in them—leashes, maybe.") There were sets and illustrated books and much-larger sections of modern firsts in bright dust jackets, gardening, art, and cookbooks. There was a children's section, and, of course, there was Bloomsbury.

At the end of May, Kevin had made a trip to London to buy books, and we arranged to meet Jocelyn at the shop when he got back. "I got some really nice things," he said when we called to make sure he'd be there. "I got a Vanessa Bell painting—on paper—and a Duncan Grant sketch of a male nude that he was going to put on a pot." He paused. "Duncan was known for his nudes, you know."

We passed along this information to Jocelyn, and told her we'd see her at the bookshop at eleven-thirty the next morning.

We got to Brick Walk about eleven. We admired the Vanessa Bell painting—at $5,000 we could admire it safely and wholeheartedly—and saw why Duncan Grant was known for his nudes. We were listening with envy to Kevin's account of his trip when Jocelyn walked in.

"Every time I meet you guys for lunch, it costs me a lot of money," she said, even before she got to us. "I never bought first editions before I met you." Then she paused and checked the time. "You got here early," she observed suspiciously.

"You're early, too."

"Not as early as you," she said.

Kevin led us over to the bookcases. There were indeed a number of new additions to the Bloomsbury section: *Violet to Vita: The Letters of Violet Trefusis to Vita Sackville-West* edited by Mitchell A. Leaska and John Phillips; *Old Friends: Portraits of a Lively Intellectual Era* by Clive Bell; *The Loving Friends: A Portrait of Bloomsbury* by David Gadd; *The Golden Echo: An Intimate Autobiography and the Portrait of a Literary Generation* by David Garnett; *Lydia & Maynard: The Letters of Lydia Lopokova and John Maynard Keynes* . . .

"Did you hear," said Jocelyn, "that there's a new book coming out that says that Virginia was actually in love with her father?"

"Why not? They're the only two left who haven't slept together."

"Very funny, Larry."

"Oh, look. Isn't that a Hogarth Press book?"

Tucked away between the biographies was a slim tan volume. The dust jacket was unmistakably Vanessa's work. Lytton Strachey and Virginia Woolf were facing each other in black silhouette, surrounded by a striking border design of black and brown. *Virginia Woolf & Lytton Strachey: Letters,* read the title. Edited by Leonard Woolf & James Strachey, The Hogarth Press. And inside, in Kevin's handwriting, "1st Edition London—1856, $125."

The preface pointed out that the letters covered a period of some twenty-five years and said that Lytton tended to keep every scrap of correspondence while Virginia was more careless; accordingly, some of the letters had been lost.

We opened the book to a random page. It was a letter by Lytton, written on Friday, November 8, 1912:

> Is it prejudice, do you think, that makes us hate the Victorians, or is it the truth of the case? They seem to me a set of mouthing bungling hypocrites; but perhaps really there is a baroque charm about them which will be discovered

> by our great-great-grandchildren, as we have discovered the charm of Donne, who seemed intolerable to the 18th century. Only I don't believe it. Thackeray and G. Meredith . . . will be curious relics in 50 years. I should like to live for another 200 years (to be moderate). The literature of the future will, I clearly see, be amazing. *At last* it'll tell the truth, and be indecent, and amusing, and romantic, and even (after about 100 years) be written well. Quelle Joie!—To live in those days, when books will pour out from the press reeking with all the filth of Petronius, all the frenzy of Dostoievsky, all the romance of the Arabian Nights, and all the exquisiteness of Voltaire!

The book was not an early Hogarth Press; it was not even exclusively a Hogarth Press; by that time Hogarth was copublishing with Chatto & Windus. Moreover, by Kevin's standards, the book was not in especially good condition. The dust jacket was slightly chipped and discolored in spots, and the book itself was worn on the edges.

None of this diminished in the least our enthusiasm to own it. It didn't seem to have much of a negative effect on Jocelyn either. She hadn't let it out of her grasp.

"You going to take it, Jocelyn?" We were all standing at the desk by now.

"Oh, no. You guys go ahead." The book, however, did not leave her hands.

"No, no. You take it."

"Oh, no, you saw it first."

"Well, we were all here together, so if you want it, Jocelyn, please, go ahead."

"No, really. You take it. I've got enough here."

"Are you sure?"

"Oh . . . yeah." She finally put the book down on the counter.

"Okay, if you really don't want it . . ." we said, quickly snatching the book up and putting it on our stack.

We all stood silently while Kevin started toting up our respective purchases.

"You're really going to take it?" asked Jocelyn.

Chapter 4

November 1, 1997

There has been a driving rain the entire day, and the journey has been harrowing. Now, with the onset of night, the rain has finally abated, reduced to a fine drizzle that leaves a mist hanging over the glistening streets. Steam rises from the entrances to the underground passageways.

The fog creates a distance, an anonymity, separating us from the other passersby. In their odd manner of dress, the custom of their native Village, they hurry along, umbrellas furled and heads down. It is dark in spite of the streetlights. There are shadows in the doorways.

In this eerie half-light, a man in a dark cape might drag a defenseless flower girl into one of those darkened doorways, and the night might then be punctuated by her single scream, and she would be past saving. Before this night is over, there will be a scream in the dark.

We arrive at our destination and make our way carefully down the stone steps. We are below street level, and the door is unlocked. We push it open and walk in.

"Good evening," breathes a short, vaguely demented-looking, completely bald man in a white shirt and a tie with a fleur-de-lis pattern overlaid with red chili peppers.

"We have reservations."

"Your name, please."

"Goldstone."

"Ah, yes. There will be four of you." He looks up from under hooded eyelids. A slightly evil grin plays at the corners of his mouth. "I've got you right here."

We have arrived early. Soon we are joined by others, a strange group indeed. We are about eighteen altogether, and included in our number is a man in his forties in skintight jeans, a torn T-shirt, a black leather jacket, and an earring; a tall woman of regal bearing in heels, escorted by a man in a tweed jacket, slacks, and sneakers; and a woman of about sixty wearing a long black dress with a rhinestone-studded choker whose hair is brushed forward in an extreme upsweep, like the wave at the opening of *Hawaii Five-O.*

However, most conspicuous is a couple who seem to have wandered in from a town in one of the remote provinces—New Canaan, Connecticut, or Upper Saddle River, New Jersey, perhaps. He is dressed in a camel-hair sports jacket, she in black-and-white-checked slacks and a blazer.

They are with us.

Suddenly, from behind the partition, there is a crash of breaking glass, followed by: AAAHHHHRRRRGGGGHHHH!!!!

Every head snaps. The woman with the hair clutches her choker. Then the slightly demented, bald-headed man with the chili-pepper tie puts up his hand. He alone has remained completely calm.

"Just a sound effect," he says with a shrug.

It was the night after Halloween, and we had come to Partners & Crime, a mystery-book store in Greenwich Village, for the Cranston and Spade Theatre Company's presentation of the WWOW Radio Mystery Hour. Instead of its usual weekend fare of "Boston Blackie" or "The Shadow," in honor of the holiday Cranston and Spade was featuring a special performance, the original Mercury Theater of the Air production of *Dracula*.

We had invited another couple, Bill and Cindy Griffeth, to join us for the evening. This was only the second time we had been out with Bill and Cindy, and the WWOW performance of *Dracula* had been our suggestion for a fun evening. When we issued the invitation, we thought ourselves terribly clever, but now, as everyone stood around in the outer room, scanning the crowd and making conversation, we began to grow more than a little apprehensive. Our selection had been as much influenced by the price of the tickets as by the subject matter—a very economical eight dollars per person, plus we got parking on the street because the meters turned off at 7 P.M. This very economy, however, was now creating some substantial anxiety. While the owners of Partners & Crime had assured us that these radio broadcasts were wonderful, now that we were actually here, it occurred to us, what else were they going to say? "Don't come, it sucks"? And if the performance wasn't any good, there was no getting away. We couldn't even duck out at intermission. From the number of people milling around, the audience was going to be far too small, and we were obviously going to be too close to the actors. A gap of four people would be yawning. Most of all, we knew that no matter how much Bill and Cindy might protest that it was certainly a good try and it wasn't our fault and it was worth the experience, if the performance turned out to be dreadful, we would forever be tainted as those morons who had suggested that weird thing in the Village.

Finally, we were allowed into the back room. It was about half the size of the one in the front. Shiny black vinyl and chrome chairs—about thirty-six altogether—had been placed in rows facing the fireplace and the narrow open space at the back that was to act as the stage. A number of chin-high microphones had been set up at the front of this stage, and, to the right, a silent, serious woman with wild, waist-length red hair tied back in a ponytail, wearing a man's shirt, tie, pants, and suspenders, topped by a Humphrey Bogart hat, was arranging an odd variety of implements including a triangle, a horn with a rubber squeeze ball at the end, a New Year's noisemaker, shoes, eggbeaters, a box with something in it that we couldn't see, a box full of silverware, chimes, a lock and key, an old-fashioned seltzer bottle, door knockers, hinges, chains, and a stapler.

The side walls were hung with old posters:

I WANT *YOU*
FOR THE U.S. ARMY

illustrated with a pointing Uncle Sam;

HOPALONG CASSIDY RADIO
CRUSHPROOF! SHATTERPROOF!
$16.95!

and;

FEARLESS FOSDICK SAYS:
GET WILDROOT
CREAM-OIL
CHARLIE!

On the wall facing all the chairs were a clock and an electric sign:

STAND BY
ON AIR

As we took our seats, several men appeared and began moving around adjusting the microphones, setting up and testing the sound system, arranging props. Suddenly, one of them turned to the others. "Give me a minute," he said. "I have to brush my teeth."

"There's something ironic about Dracula having to brush his teeth," noted one of the other men as the first disappeared offstage.

As a testament to our state of mind, we chose seats in the back row.

Seated directly in front of us on the aisle was an attractive woman in her early fifties with short red curly hair and jeans. Soon after we sat down, an artistic-looking dark-haired man in his forties squeezed past her and took the chair two seats away. For the next few minutes they occupied themselves by glancing at their programs and occasionally at one another. Finally, the man leaned toward the woman, draping his arm over the empty chair between them.

"Do you think we are limited?" he asked.

"No," she replied.

"I'm a filmmaker," said the man, "and I think we must be."

"Are you sure?" the woman asked.

"Yes," replied the man.

The woman considered this. "Why can't we *pretend* we're limitless?" she asked, throwing out one arm.

"That's a very refreshing thing to hear," said the man. "I *feel* so limited."

"I'm a naturally funny person," confided the woman.

The man nodded slowly. "All good comedy is based on pain," he said.

It was at this moment that the lights went out.

"Stand by," said a woman's voice into a microphone.

ON AIR, blinked the sign.

The man with the chili-pepper tie stepped up to a microphone in the center as the other actors took their places. The men were dressed in 1940s suits. A woman wore a hat with a veil. Synthesized organ music filled the room.

"And now . . . *Dracula*."

We might never have walked into a mystery-book store at all had not Partners & Crime called our publisher a few months earlier to ask us to do a reading and signing for *Used and Rare*. Although we accepted the offer with alacrity—it was the only request we had had to sign books in Manhattan—we were also confused. What did a shop that specialized in serial killers or old-lady amateur sleuths want with two writers who had just published a memoir about book collecting?

"Are they going to get any people to come to this?" we asked our publicist.

"Oh yes," she assured us breezily. "They have a big mailing list."

Although the public conception of a book signing is a partylike event where a heavily promoted celebrity like Judith Krantz or Colin Powell holds court while a line of people stretches out the door, waiting patiently for their moment with the author, the reality for 99.9 percent of writers is somewhat different. At most book signings, an author will be lucky to sign five copies. Oftentimes, even at a bookstore with "a big mailing list," you can sit for two hours at a desk at the front of the store with a large poster beside you and a stack of books next to you without a single person even stopping to inquire about the work, let alone buy the book.

This happened to a friend of ours at a chain bookstore outlet at a shopping center. He had been sitting completely alone for ninety minutes (after ten minutes, the aura of failure is so intense at these affairs that even the store employees withdraw to the safety of the checkout counter) when a woman with a child finally approached him. She looked both ways and then leaned over slightly.

"Are you a writer?" she asked.

"Yes," said our friend.

"You wrote this book?"

Our friend assured her that he had.

"I have to do some shopping at the store across the way," she said. "Would you mind watching my son for a few minutes?"

So we had come to understand that if we agreed to a signing, we had better be prepared to supply most of the crowd ourselves. The problem was we hadn't lived in New York for almost ten years. We unearthed a decade-old address book and proceeded to send a postcard announcement to every single person listed therein, including a number of people who we felt sure loathed us.

On the night of the signing, we got to Partners & Crime about a half hour early. Usually when you do one of these, you have to find whoever is in charge of community relations at the bookstore and introduce yourself. In this case, however, as soon as we walked in the door, a tall, lean, red-haired man in his forties with long thin sideburns that curved slightly forward and tapered into points like apostrophes, and wearing leather pants, strode in our direction with a smile on his face.

"You must be the Goldstones," he said. "I'm John Douglas, one of the partners here. We're so glad to have you. I loved your book."

We thanked him (profusely) then looked around. Partners & Crime was a large open room with floor-to-ceiling shelves lining the walls and some free-standing bookcases set on angles in the middle of the room. There were an old loveseat and some worn chairs sprinkled about for comfortable browsing. It looked just like a regular independent bookstore—or at least what independent bookstores used to look like before they all closed—except that this store specialized in mysteries. We were surprised that, except for one or two big names like Patricia Cornwell or Robert B. Parker, we didn't recognize a single author. Who was Laurie R. King or Mercedes Lambert? What about Nancy Atherton and *Aunt Dimity's Good Deed*? Death was popular in titles. There were *Rueful Death, Death at the Wheel, Death in Little Tokyo,* and *The Death of an Irish Sea Wolf.* The new nonfiction section was different, too. It contained histories of mysteries, biographies of famous mystery writers, magazines for mystery lovers, and true-crime titles like *Kill Grandma for Me* and *Bulletproof Diva: Tales of Race, Sex, and Hair.*

The self-help section consisted of a series of manuals that detailed police procedures, forensics, murder weapons and methodology—all the neat ways that one person could dispose of another—and handbooks containing job descriptions at various law-enforcement agencies and sample tests for obtaining employment. Inside the handbooks were questions like:

> A police department purchases badges at $16 each for all the graduates of the police training academy. The last training class graduated 10 new officers. What is the total amount of money the department will spend for badges for these new officers?
> (A) $70
> (B) $116
> (C) $160
> (D) $180
> (E) None of these
> The correct response is **C**. It can be obtained by computing the following: 16 × 10 = 160

"Why don't you come back here where we set up?" said John.

We followed him to the rear of the store. There was a fireplace against the back wall, flanked by glass-fronted bookcases, with a couch in front and about thirty folding chairs set up facing it. There was a little table to the side of the couch with a pitcher of water, two glasses, and a microphone.

We walked over to check out the couch, but instead our eyes were drawn to the books in the glass-fronted cases. They were mostly mysteries with some literature mixed in. But they were not new books. They were out-of-print first editions, most in excellent condition, some of them in the hundred-dollar-plus range. We saw firsts of Ian Fleming, Erle Stanley Gardner, and John LeCarré, works of classic mystery writers like Patricia Highsmith, Michael

Innes, and George Simenon, as well as books by Erica Jong and Thomas Pynchon.

"Collectors are a big part of our business," noted John Douglas. "Jon handles them."

"Aren't you John?"

"Jon Teta. He's another partner. We have two Maggies, too. And a Kizmin. It's like a five-way marriage around here sometimes," he said.

Suddenly we noticed a book on the shelf that didn't seem to belong there. It was a first edition, all right, and even a mystery. What made it stand out was that it usually sold for about seven hundred dollars.

"You've got *Booked To Die*?" we asked, pulling the book out. The dust jacket was pristine. "How much is it?"

"I'm not sure," said John Douglas. "Teta!" he called. "How much is *Booked to Die*?"

Jon Teta was behind the front desk. He was a balding, fiftyish man with a furry mustache, wearing a plaid shirt. "It's a hundred."

Before we could snap, "We'll take it!" Teta added, "It's missing a front endpaper."

Booked To Die was a hard-boiled detective novel by John Dunning published in 1992. Along with *Postmortem,* Patricia Cornwell's first book, and Sue Grafton's *"A" Is for Alibi,* it was one of a handful of recent mysteries of which we were aware whose prices had skyrocketed. Either of those two can sell for over one thousand dollars. But, where Cornwell's Kay Scarpetta and Grafton's Kinsey Millhone went on to long and hugely popular careers, Dunning's Cliff Janeway appeared in just one more book. What makes a Janeway book valuable is that, in addition to his detecting, he was also a book collector, and Dunning is an antiquarian book dealer in Denver. It is the wealth of detail about Janeway's book-craft, rather than his cop-craft, that gives *Booked To Die* its appeal.

We turned the book over in our hands. The front of the dust jacket had a picture of bookshelves in a used-book store with the shadow of a hulking man falling from right to left in front of a table in the back labeled "Discount Books." On the back cover, in the place where the quotes or reviews usually go was:

A RARE BOOK QUIZ
FROM BOOKED TO DIE AUTHOR
JOHN DUNNING

1. Seventeen years ago it was a 99-cent remainder book on chain store sale tables. Today it sells for $200.
   a. *The Honorary Consul,* by Graham Greene
   b. *Nickel Mountain,* by John Gardner
   c. *The Milagro Beanfield War,* by John Nichols
   d. *The World of Apples,* by John Cheever
2. Name the $1,000 book in fine first edition.
   a. *Intruder in the Dust,* by William Faulkner
   b. *The Lady in the Lake,* by Raymond Chandler
   c. *For Whom the Bell Tolls,* by Ernest Hemingway
   d. *Pudd'nhead Wilson,* by Mark Twain
3. What book was recently found in a used book store bin for $15 and sold at auction for almost $250,000?
   a. *Moby Dick,* by Herman Melville
   b. *Tamerlane,* by A Bostonian
   c. *Birds of America,* by John James Audubon
   d. *Incidents of Travel in the Yucatan,* by John L. Stephens, 1843, with an original map
4. Name the $3,000 book.
   a. *Lord of the Flies,* first American edition, by William Golding
   b. *Interview with the Vampire,* by Anne Rice
   c. *Firestarter,* limited edition of 26 copies by Stephen King
   d. *Knave of Hearts,* by Louise Saunders, with illustrations by Maxfield Parrish

Underneath was written: "Read *Booked To Die* to discover the sometimes surprising answers!"

We took the book up to the front. "We'll take it," we said.

"You saw the endpaper?" asked Jon Teta.

"Yes. But the dust jacket is perfect. One of these days we'll see a copy without a dust jacket for fifty dollars. Then, for a hundred and fifty, we'll have a seven-hundred-dollar book."

Teta nodded. "Yep. That's right."

As he started to ring it up, we asked, "Do most of the people who come in here collect?"

"Some," he replied, "but mostly we get people who are looking for a good read that they might not have found otherwise. The first question everyone who walks in here asks is 'What do you recommend?' Each of us reads three or four books a week, and our customers know it. They're not looking for blockbusters . . . we don't carry more than two or three copies of John Grisham here . . . he doesn't sell."

John D. wandered up to join us. "Also, we thought there should be a place where the public could come into contact with all aspects of crime writing," he said. "Someplace where they could interact with professionals, not just get their signatures.

"So, in addition to signings, we hold a bunch of events here—how to write a mystery, how to get your first book published, how to get a mystery published, how to get a short story published. We get agents and editors and writers like Walter Mosley, P. D. James, and Anne Perry to come here and talk."

Soon after, people started drifting in. Including a few Connecticut friends who work in the city, we ended up with about fifteen people. They were attentive, interested, asked intelligent questions, and seemed to have a good time. As a result, so did we.

We even had a score from the postcards we'd sent out. It was Bill Griffeth, a daytime anchor for CNBC, who covers the financial markets. Bill, at the time, was the most casual of acquaintances. We'd only come in contact with him once, in 1988, when he was with FNN and conducted a three-minute interview with Nancy, who had just written a book called *Trading Up,* the true account of her experiences as a completely unqualified twenty-seven-year-old who got to be the head currency-options trader for a major bank.

It turned out that Bill loved books and had a small collection of his own. He specialized in astronomy and John Fowles.

On our way out, we stopped at the front desk one last time. They had a bunch of 5 × 7 postcards in different colors announcing upcoming events on the counter. There were two, the red and the yellow, that caught our eye. The red one gave the dates and the programs for upcoming performances of the WWOW Mystery Hour.

"Oh, they're excellent," said Jon Teta. "At our very first meeting, I sat there and said that there was no way for an independent bookstore to survive based simply on the retail end. If we were going to do this, we were going to have to find ways to open up the walls. We had to have some way, for example, to get theater involved. Those bookshelves," he said, pointing to the walls at the rear, "are actually rolling partitions that we swing forward on the weekends to make a back room for the show."

The yellow card read:

SISTERS IN CRIME NY/TRI-STATE
5:30 p.m.—Partners & Crime

How Far Will You Go For Research?
Audiotape of Actual Human Autopsy
Filmed by Baltimore Medical Examiner's Office
In association with the "Homicide" television series.
This tape includes footage of the crime scene
as well as the full autopsy itself.
Almost as good—or bad—as Being There

7:30 Dinner (optional)

"Sisters in Crime? What are they . . . nuns?"

"No, no," said John Douglas. "They're women crime writers. It's a national organization. This is the local chapter."

"And where do they go for dinner?"

"I hope to a vegetarian restaurant," he replied.

Now aware that mystery-book stores also carried used books, to say nothing of staging some unusual events, we decided to check out some others. There were three other mystery-book stores in Manhattan: the Mysterious Book Shop near Carnegie Hall, Black Orchid on the East Side, and Murder Ink on Ninety-third and Broadway.

Murder Ink was a crisp, clean store about half the size of Partners & Crime. There was a distinct background odor of Chinese food. It had a number of new hardcover mysteries on a table in the front, many of them marked "signed," and wraparound bookshelves filled with other hardcovers and paperbacks. In the back, in an alcove on the right, was an entire section devoted to first editions of out-of-print books. We saw immediately that this selection was older, more extensive, and more valuable than the one we had seen at Partners & Crime, with authors that you don't see very often in first edition, like S. S. Van Dine, Ellery Queen, James M. Cain, Rex Stout, Mickey Spillane, and W. R. Burnett. It was as fine a selection as could be found in any antiquarian bookstore.

"Is collecting a big part of your business?" we asked Diane Plumley, who managed the store.

Diane was in her thirties with long blonde hair. She was wearing a T-shirt with a full-color picture of the head of what appeared to be a malevolent ferret. When she spoke, she radiated the combination of ingenuousness and vague New York cynicism that Woody Allen has been making a living off of for years.

"Oh, yeah," she said. "We have a lot of collectors. We just bought about two thousand books from the Carter Burden estate. Jay—he's the owner, Jay Pearsall—has a real vision for the store. He's the one who knows about this stuff. I do more hypermoderns."

Hypermoderns was a term that we had begun to encounter with more and more frequency. We had first heard it about a year earlier from Peter Stern of Peter Stern Books in Boston. When we'd questioned him about the four-figure price fetched by *"A" Is for Alibi,* Peter, who knows as much about modern firsts as anyone, had waved his hand dismissively and said, "Ach, I don't know anything about hypermoderns."

Since then, however, we had noticed that some books that were not very old had begun to appreciate in price way out of proportion to what seemed to be their underlying value. For example, a book called *Snow Falling on Cedars* by David Guterson, which we had bought new for $19 at Barnes & Noble in 1996 because some guy at the gym thought it was wonderful, to our pleased amazement was now listed regularly in dealer catalogs at $125 or $150, and we had seen signed copies listed for upwards of $200.

"That's what our customers want," said Diane firmly. "Signed firsts. We don't really do events here. We don't have the space like Partners. We just get the authors in here to sign their books.

"My thing is I have the knack for knowing what's going to make it," she continued. "I get the publishers' catalogs, and I look through them, and a lot of the time I know what's worth having and what isn't. For example, last year I saw *An Embarrassment of Corpses* by Alan Beechey. I read it. It was wonderful. The first printing was only twenty-five hundred books. He had to sell it out to get a sequel, and I was determined to do that for him even if I had to call twenty-five hundred people myself."

She pointed to her T-shirt. "It's Finsbury," she said and explained that Finsbury the Ferret was a foul-mouthed, cigarette-smoking, thoroughly disreputable children's book character who played a significant role in *An Embarrassment of Corpses.*

The hypermodern market, which is perhaps the hottest area of book collecting today, while not exclusively mysteries, is primarily mystery driven. This is a function of the economics of mystery publishing, which, in turn, is a function of some unusual properties of the mystery reader.

People who read mysteries are not like other readers. Many of them read nothing else. A sizable number, we have been told, don't have or watch television. They are demanding of plot and structure and often develop a maniacal devotion to a favorite character. Everyone knows that there are Sherlock Holmes societies all over the world, but it goes way beyond that. Almost every long-running fictional detective has his or her own cadre of fanatics, those who have not only read every book or story in which their hero appears, but who also correspond with each other, speculate about minute omissions or inconsistencies in the stories (often nothing more than oversights by the writer), and spend a good deal of time trying to fill in those parts of the detective's life unspecified by his or her creator.

As a result, successful mystery writers often become slaves to their inventions, like the dummy-dominated ventriloquist in *Dead of Night*. Arthur Conan Doyle grew to detest being limited to one character and made any number of efforts to bury Sherlock Holmes, even resorting once to killing him by pushing him over a waterfall. Nothing worked. Giving in to public outcry, Doyle was forced to bring Holmes back from the dead.

Even today, mega-stars like Patricia Cornwell are not allowed to just end a series when they think a character is worn out. We were at a signing at Black Orchid, the mystery-book store on East Eighty-third Street, when we saw a woman pick up a copy of *Hornet's Nest,* which, at the time, was Cornwell's latest.

"What do you think of this one?" she asked Joe Gugliemielli, who along with Bonnie Claeson owns Black Orchid.

"I liked it," replied Joe, a large, affable former lawyer, "but a lot of people were upset that she didn't keep up the Kay Scarpetta series."

"Really?" the woman replied, looking stricken. "Kay Scarpetta isn't in this one at all?"

Joe shook his head.

The woman immediately put *Hornet's Nest* back on the shelf.

For new writers the pressures are, if anything, more intense.

Fans, and by extension publishers, demand that every new mystery be the first of a potential series. The stakes here are enormous. A series can run to ten, even twenty books, and when a Sue Grafton or a Patricia Cornwell or a Dick Francis publishes a new book, and they do a new one almost every year, a publisher can count on hundreds of thousands of copies in hardcover. With the rewards of a successful mystery series so immense, many mystery publishers, unlike publishers in other areas of the industry, are willing, even eager, to publish new authors. The risk is minimal—these new authors get small printings and even smaller publicity budgets. If only one out of one hundred in this literary lottery catches on, even a little, it will more than cover the expenditures on the other ninety-nine. Thus Alan Beechey, having sold his 2,500 books (in no small part due to Diane Plumley's efforts), is already ahead of the game.

But Charles Todd is an even better example. Todd's first book, *A Test of Wills,* was published in 1996, also with a first printing of around 2,500 books. Unlike *An Embarrassment of Corpses,* however, *A Test of Wills* acquired an instant following. It was nominated for an Edgar Award as Best First Mystery, and had at least four printings in hardcover.

A Test of Wills was set in a small English country town in the years immediately following World War I, and introduced Inspector Ian Rutledge, a Scotland Yard investigator and war veteran who was now back on the job after a severe case of shell shock. Although pronounced cured by army doctors, he still occasionally heard the mocking voice of Hamish, a Scottish private Rutledge had been forced to execute for cowardice on the battlefield. Given this symptom, shell shock was, not surprisingly, generally viewed as a form of mental illness in 1919, so Rutledge, in addition to solving the crime, must maneuver to keep his medical history a secret.

The success of *A Test of Wills* resulted in a contract for an additional three books with the potential for a good many beyond that. *Wings of Fire,* the second in the series, had an announced first printing of 17,500 books, and Todd got an author tour.

Originally, Todd wasn't sure what to do about Hamish as the series progressed. After all, it might get tiresome by the tenth book to always have this disembodied voice popping up at odd places. Then, too, the presence of Hamish would mean that Rutledge had not recovered from his war illness, which, if the series eventually moved on to, say, 1930, might also become a bit unwieldy. Maggie Griffin, one of the Maggies from Partners & Crime, and a friend of Todd's, suggested to him that Hamish be phased out in later books, to indicate Rutledge's eventual recovery. But no, that wasn't going to be possible. So vociferous were Todd's fans that he was forced to publicly promise that Hamish would appear in every Rutledge story.

Now, with the potential of a long series in sight, and a tiny first printing of the first of the series, Charles Todd said that he had personally seen a signed first edition of *A Test of Wills* priced at $260 less than one year after it had been published.

Most book collectors are not used to the potential of 1,000 percent run-ups in a year, and handle the stress in different ways. There are those who simply buy every single new mystery published in hardcover. Most others, however, try to find ways to be a bit more selective.

Each of the mystery-book stores has a mailing list and produces either a newsletter or a catalog in which it lists the staff recommendations. These recommendations carry far more weight than simply identifying what's good to read. The recommendation of someone like Diane Plumley, for example, is viewed almost as inside information. "If I even say this *could* be a collectible book, it gets way out of hand," said Diane.

In addition to mystery-book store recommendations, the hypermodern market has its own tip sheet.

"I look for books with modest first printings (generally) that attract a lot more attention than expected by the publisher. I look for strong first books that will rise in value as a successful career is built. I look for strong reviews from the prepublication sources, and a 'buzz.' The most important consideration is generally word of mouth. The whole idea is to point folks towards a title that might really catch on before they have to pay some dealer fifty dollars for it," said David M. Brown.

David is the owner and publisher of Book*Line,* "The Premiere Newsletter for Collectors of Mystery and Suspense Fiction." (He also has a newsletter for modern firsts and literature.) He is forty years old and graduated from Bowling Green University with a BS in finance and accounting. Before Book*Line* he worked for a couple of mutual funds and a small investment firm in California.

"I broke all the rules for launching a newsletter," he said. "I had literally a handful of subscribers at the beginning. The newsletter continues to grow, but we seem to have picked up more influence than our subscription numbers would suggest.

"The first book that made me a collector was *Shoeless Joe* by W. P. Kinsella. I remember buying several copies of that book and giving them away to friends because I thought it was so wonderful. Baseball and literature are a lethal combination for me. While I think that book made me a collector, I don't own a single copy. I gave them all away, and then when the book moved up in price, I never replaced my own copy. Still, that imprinted a bit of bibliomania on me. I started paying attention. I made sure to get a first edition of a book that interested me when it came out, and I learned how to take care of my books."

"People are buying mostly for the wrong reasons," said Otto Penzler flatly. "They're buying for an investment. They only think about *Postmortem* going for one thousand dollars. They don't think about *Dog Town. Dog Town* is by Mercedes Lambert. It was a hugely hot book at the time, but now you can buy it for two dollars."

Otto Penzler is the Zeus of the mystery-book world. He's fiftyish, with meticulously groomed white hair, a white beard, and piercing blue eyes—perfect for Zeus. He is the owner of The Mysterious Book Shop, a two-story brownstone on West Fifty-sixth Street. In addition to the shop, he was the founder of the Mysterious Press, which became so successful that it was the object of a corporate takeover by Warner Books. He has published a number of recent anthologies, is an archivist, and has produced scrupulously accurate facsimile editions of such classics as *The Big Sleep* and *The Maltese Falcon* that, if not for one small notation on the dust jacket and one on the copyright page, would be indistinguishable from the originals. His personal collection of mysteries runs to over thirty thousand books and is certainly one of the finest and most complete in the world. Some of the collection is housed in his private office at the second-floor rear of the shop on twelve-foot floor-to-ceiling bookshelves that were built for him nail by nail by such mystery legends as Ed McBain, Donald E. Westlake, and Lawrence Block. In a business in which just about everyone else is scraping by, happy to make enough money just to cover expenses, Otto Penzler is *rich*. His name is spoken with a combination of fear, envy, and reverence by other people in the business.

"I've been collecting for thirty years," he said. "For the last twelve years, I've collected every mystery that comes out. Before that, I collected nineteenth-century mysteries. I got started when I was working at the *Daily News* as a copyboy earning forty-two dollars a week. There was a bookshop across the street on Forty-third called James Drake. One day I walked in just because it looked interesting."

We were sitting in Otto's office; it's the kind of room that makes you gasp. Those twelve-foot shelves surround you, so everywhere you look there are books, thousands upon thousands of them, one priceless first edition after another, with additional bookcases in the middle of the floor, along with tables heaped with books, and even piles of books on the oriental carpet. It was dim, with just an overhanging globe light and a lamp on a table. All the colors were dark brown or red—a deep red oriental rug, a dark red leather couch, a red armchair, a dark brown armchair, dark wood paneling.

"The man who owned it was quite elderly at the time . . . his father had founded the store," Otto continued. "I always called him Mr. Drake. I was young, and I had alloted myself a budget of five dollars a week for books. I would go into Mr. Drake's store, and there were first editions of Kipling and Keats and so on, which at the time went for five dollars, so I bought them. I did this regularly, once a week, and I talked to old Mr. Drake. Of course, in the back he had ten-thousand-dollar books, but I didn't know that.

"Then, one day, I pulled a book off the shelf, and he said, 'You know, I have a much better copy of that book in the back, but it's twice as much.'

" 'I can't afford that,' I said.

" 'Well,' said Mr. Drake, 'you could if you don't buy a book this week. I could put the book away for you, and then next week, you'd have ten dollars to spend, and you could buy the book.'

"He said, 'Of course, it's your choice, but condition really makes a difference.' So I bought the book. Mr. Drake was my Book Collecting 101 course.

"Mr. Drake started putting books away for me. I was young, and I guess he liked me. Then one day he said, 'I have a great book for you. A signed first edition of *The Picture of Dorian Gray*. But it's twenty dollars.'

"I hesitated. 'Is it a good book?' I asked finally. Twenty dollars was a lot of money.

" 'Oh, yes,' Mr. Drake assured me. 'It's a very good book. Don't worry. You'll like it.'

"What I didn't know at the time was that Mr. Drake was getting older and getting ready to leave the business and *The Picture of Dorian Gray* was a five-hundred-dollar book that he was selling me for twenty dollars."

At a time when almost everyone who collected was wealthy and trading in first editions of Dashiell Hammett, Sherlock Holmes, or

Wilkie Collins, Otto Penzler was either the first or one of the first people to recognize that someone who wasn't rich could create a collection by purchasing books as they came out, before they had a chance to appreciate in value.

"I used to do a column for *Ellery Queen Mystery Magazine,*" said Otto. "If I was going to interview someone like Donald Westlake, for example, I'd take along a few first editions and have him sign them.

"So when I opened my store nineteen years ago, we had first editions and got people started. That's when it started to take off . . . I had an influence on *collecting,* I was paying attention to *collectors,* not readers—not the paperback people. Literature is too broadly defined to pick and choose for other people. Mystery is narrow enough to have a focus.

"Then I started a book club. Everybody does it now, but I was the first one. Once a month, my customers got an autographed first edition in the mail if they signed up. Robert B. Parker's new book at cover price, for example. But it wasn't that easy to get signed copies. Mystery authors didn't tour twenty years ago. We had trouble getting twelve authors a year."

Otto laughed. "Seems kind of funny now, doesn't it?"

Otto Penzler is not alone in making the distinction between serious collecting and the buying up willy-nilly of books by untested authors in the hope that one day, very soon, the price will jump.

"Books today become valuable so quickly, but for what? For about ten seconds," said Diane Plumley.

Jon Teta agreed. "I always tell people, 'Collect what you like.' If you're in this for the investment—forget about it. It's the worst investment."

Heeding this advice, we have made it a point to avoid hypermoderns, although that does not stop us, when buying a new book, from going to as many bookstores as it takes until we find a first edition.

It started with music. It was synthesized organ music, nice and creepy. A man stepped forward. He was of medium height, appeared to be in his midforties, and was wearing a conservative gray pin-striped business suit that fit imperfectly. He looked as though he had just come from working a day job at the IRS.

"I am Jonathan Harker," he said in a hushed voice, "and I swear that the events I am about to describe are true . . ."

As Jonathan Harker described his carriage journey to Count Dracula's castle, the whole atmosphere was so right that you just wanted to close your eyes to get the full flavor of radio. But you couldn't, because what was going on on stage was too interesting to miss.

They were all good, but the person to watch was the woman in the Bogart hat with the long red hair. She did the sound effects. She clomped the shoes in the box of broken glass, blew the train whistle, rapped hollow cups to make the sound of horses' hooves at Borgo Pass, and popped balloons with a dart for gunshots. She had a copy of the script in front of her and never seemed to take her eyes off it, while her hands moved expertly from a kitchen utensil to a pencil sharpener. When the carriage carrying Jonathan Harker was clattering across the countryside heading toward Dracula's castle, she suddenly turned her head toward a corner of the wall, and the sound of a pack of baying wolves filled the room. It was only after a couple more wolf howls that we realized that the sound-effects woman was creating them, not with an implement, but with her voice. We also realized that the reason she turned her head to the wall was to bounce the sound, thus making the wolves' howls seem appropriately far off.

When the lights went on at the end of the performance, the troupe got a standing ovation. Theater in New York has become so spotty and so expensive that it is rare that an entire audience, regardless of its size, leaves the room so obviously happy, but that is what happened here. A couple of people even bought books on the way out.

Flushed with success, we took Bill and Cindy around the corner to Indigo, a hip new restaurant that we had located on the Internet. Indigo was hopping. The food was great, the waitress was professional—friendly and wearing so many studs that she was probably setting off metal detectors at all three major New York airports from where she stood—and no one seemed to mind that we were, by about twenty years, the oldest people in the place.

After dinner, we all parted in the best of moods, shaking hands, kissing, and vowing to do something just as much fun next time.

Hey! What about Sisters in Crime?

Chapter 5

We were browsing at Howard S. Mott Rare Books in Sheffield, Massachusetts, a few years ago when one of us saw a book, worn and faded, with a once–forest green binding. It was entitled *Cudjo's Cave,* and on the spine, under the title, instead of a name, it read, "by the author of *Neighbor Jackwood.*"

"Nancy! Come here!"

"What?"

"Look. A book about Cudjo."

"Who's Cudjo?"

"Who's Cudjo? Who's Cudjo? Don't you know anything? He was a freedom fighter, one of the greatest military minds in history. He was like, I don't know . . . George Washington . . . Nelson Mandela . . . Ho Chi Minh . . ."

"Oh, *that* Cudjo."

"Yeah, yeah. I never knew anyone had written a book about him, though."

Sure enough, leafing through quickly, there was indeed a character named Cudjo who had taken refuge in a cave to wage war against his oppressors. There was also an inscription on the front endpaper, written with a fountain pen in tiny, perfectly formed letters, that read, "Grandmother Stoddard to Lizzie. For doing an errand for her. Aug 17, 1872." It was only on the title page that the author's name, J. T. Trowbridge, finally appeared. *Cudjo's Cave* had been published in Boston by J. E. Tilton and Company in 1864.

"Nancy, can you believe this? Someone in Boston, at the height of the Civil War, wrote an historical novel depicting one of the great guerrilla campaigns in history, a campaign that had begun almost two centuries before and was virtually unknown outside the country in which it had occurred?"

"How much?"

"Thirteen dollars! It isn't a first. For Cudjo. Ha, ha ha. What a deal!"

We got back in the car to drive home. There was still a good deal of chortling coming from the driver's side.

"All right, Larry. I give up. What's so special about Cudjo?"

"Well, Nancy, it was before we met."

"Really? I didn't think you did anything interesting before we met."

"Only this once. It was back in the early eighties. I wanted to go on vacation to someplace a little unusual . . ."

Flashback: New York City, late December 1983. Norman's office.

"Have you ever been to Jamaica?" inquired Norman. Norman had dark hair and the sort of pencil mustache that one generally associates with 1930s porn films, the ones in which the male lead always wore black socks. Norman was a travel agent.

"The atmosphere is totally changed since Manley was voted out," he went on, sifting through a file. "They're trying everything to attract tourists. Maybe a small, elegant hotel, off the beaten track?" After a few moments, he unearthed a brochure and handed it across the desk.

It was one of those small, fold-out affairs with three sections. "Miranda Hill" was written across the front, and underneath was a photograph of a smiling, long-legged brunette in a two-piece bathing suit stretched languorously across a king-size bed. The bathing suit and the hair looked kind of sixties, but the room was large and sumptuous, with double French doors that opened out on to the pool.

"It's in Montego Bay," Norman explained. "Small, very chic, away from the Holiday Inn and all the tourist spots. Private, too. You won't be bothered by other guests."

Norman was right. I wasn't bothered by other guests. There were no other guests.

When the photograph on the brochure was taken, Miranda Hill doubtless had been elegant and very chic. The ensuing twenty years, however, had witnessed a number of changes. Most significantly, the hotel had been sold. The new owners were a gang of *ganga* smugglers.

Although, for some obscure reason, Miranda Hill continued to function as a bona fide hotel, the management, while completely hospitable, was not especially aggressive about attracting a tourist trade. The only foreigners who did show up apparently did so on the basis of that same twenty-year-old brochure that had so captivated Norman. Miranda Hill's main function these days, it seemed, was to supply comfortable, readily available accommodations for family, friends, and business associates of the gang members. Every evening, anyone who fell into one or more of these categories gathered around the pool, lit spliffs as thick as chicken legs, and proceeded to send enormous clouds of marijuana smoke off into the night.

The staff was either oblivious or unaffected by the shift in clientele. Every morning, crisply dressed maids, grounds keepers, front desk personnel, and kitchen staff scurried about (by Jamaican standards) as if the place were still filled with Wall Streeters and Eurotrash.

Amazingly, the food was first-rate. Aki (a fruit that cooks up like scrambled eggs) for breakfast and grilled snapper or dolphin (the fish, not Flipper) with banana for dinner. The wait-staff was attentive and courteous and consisted of Smitty, who was on duty for every meal, every day. Smitty was about fifty, stocky but not fat, with graying hair and muttonchop sideburns. Like most people on the island, he provided any variety of services, information, and spiritual insights that might enable him to scratch out a modest living.

On January 6, at breakfast, he leaned down and made a proposal.

"Ever hear of 'Compong?"

"No."

" 'Compong Town in de hills, mon. Every year dey have a big fest-i-val. What about if I take you?"

That meant he had no money to go himself. "What kind of festival?"

"Cudjo's birthday, mon. Is big do-ins. Folks from all over de is-land come."

"Sounds good. How do we get there?"

"Got to rent a taxi."

That figured. "How far is 'Compong?"

Smitty rubbed his chin. Measure of distances tends to be somewhat subjective in Jamaica. "Not too far."

Smitty was technically correct. 'Compong (actually Accompong, as both the town and the festival are known) was only about thirty miles away.

At seven the next morning we secured our taxi. First, we drove to Magotty, a mining town in the center of the island. This portion of the trip was the standard Jamaican ride in the country—two-lane highway, passes on blind curves, and screeching brakes intermixed with space-shot-caliber acceleration. That left the short jaunt from Magotty to Accompong Town, only six miles as the crow flies. Unfortunately, the crow would have to fly straight up. For humans, it meant negotiating a narrow, winding, unpaved mountain road.

Until the early 1960s, this road was for horses and mules only and even by the 1980s had been upgraded not a whit to accommodate vehicular traffic. It was an utterly unique experience to be on the outside when two cars had to pass in opposite directions.

None of this perturbed Smitty in the least. The idea of plunging hundreds of feet down a rocky hillside to certain and horrible death seemed to have no effect on him whatever.

"I be only half Ma-roon, you know," he said. "Dat mean I cannot go into de cave."

"What cave?"

"Cudjo's cave, mon," he replied, as if he had just been asked the dumbest question in the entire world. "It where dey hole up when de redcoats come. Dey cannot get him out no way. Dat because of de spir-rits. Now only full-blooded Ma-roons can go. I be only half Ma-roon."

"Uh, what are Maroons?"

Smitty stared. "Dey runaway slaves, mon. Fight de British for hundred years. Cudjo de lea-der. Den de British give up. Sign a trea-ty. Make Ma-roonland a free na-tion. 'Compong Town de capital. De trea-ty still in de colonel's house." Smitty paused and wrinkled his brows. Just yesterday he had confided that he had never heard of Ronald Reagan. "Don' dey teach you not-ting in school?"

The thirty miles took four hours. When we reached Accompong Town, the festival was in full swing. Rastamen listening to Bob Marley or Toots and the Maytalls on boom boxes walked past school girls twirling ribbons around a maypole. Visitors, who numbered in the hundreds and virtually all of whom were Jamaican—there were less than five other white faces in the whole place—strolled the grounds chatting, eating, and looking utterly content. The one or two policemen stood by as spliffs were openly smoked and passed.

"On Cudjo's birthday, *ganga* le-gal," Smitty noted.

The most amazing sight, however, was that of two immense stretch limousines parked in the open field that was the town square and a tall, thin, distinguished, silver-haired man in a dark suit who looked a lot like Mountbatten, chatting with some revelers.

"Dat de gover-nor," said Smitty. "He come all de way from King-ston. I tol' you. 'Compong big do-ins."

"How did the cars get here?" I asked.

"Same way we did, mon. Only one road." Smitty started heading off toward the edge of the town. "Come on den. We go to my aunt's house. She de bes' cook in Ma-roonland."

Smitty's aunt's house turned out to be a shack propped up on piles of unmortared bricks. It was about twenty feet square and housed Smitty's aunt, Smitty's aunt's current man, Smitty's aunt's four children, and four or five other people whose origins were undesignated. The front door, which swung freely on rusted hinges, had no lock.

Just behind the house was a stretch of open country as far as the eye could see. Not a single structure was visible. The ground was teeming with huge sinkholes as if some Ashanti or Coramantee god had peppered the ground with giant buckshot.

"Dat cockpit country," Smitty explained. "Where Cudjo and his men cover demselves wit' leaves an' mud and ambush de redcoats." He turned back to the house. "First we eat some lunch, den I take you to meet de colonel."

There was a large pot hanging over an open fire. Smitty's aunt was ladling out some brothy mixture into large bowls when we came up. She was a small, remarkably attractive woman wearing a flowered bandana on her head who looked to be about forty, although Smitty swore she was over sixty.

"Dis here 'po'r water,' " said Smitty, pointing to the pot. "My aunt de bes' cook in Ma-roonland."

" 'Po'r water?' "

"Yah, mon. Goat's head soup."

Goat's head soup. Smitty's aunt was already ladling. She said something in an indecipherable patois. Smitty had mentioned that folks in 'Compong Town spoke in a dialect that even he had trouble understanding.

"My aunt want to know if you want de brains." He nodded respectfully. "Dat de best part."

"Uh, thanks, but that's not necessary."

Smitty shrugged. His aunt finished ladling, then handed out some warm, freshly baked bread, and we all sat down to eat.

There was not the tiniest possibility of begging off. It was not even the question of running afoul of Smitty and his aunt and ending up marooned in Maroonland. It was simply unthinkable to insult people who were, for no other reason than that they wanted to, treating someone whom they had never met before more cordially and hospitably than most in-laws. I took a breath, pasted on a crooked smile, and dug in.

It was *great.*

The broth was thick and sweet, the onions, potatoes, and carrots done perfectly, and even the small pieces of meat (think meat, not goat) tender and delicious. Smitty's aunt (she was never referred to as anything else) smiled beatifically as each spoonful went down.

After Smitty finished his third helping, he sat back and patted his stomach. He looked ready to settle in for a nap when, suddenly, he remembered his obli-ga-tions and sat up.

"Come on," he said, torturously pushing himself erect. "Time to go see de colonel."

"The colonel" was the governor of Maroonland. It was unclear if he was appointed or elected. He lived in a small house in the center of town that was distinguished from the rest of the dwellings by what may have been the only door lock in all Accompong and the presence of a screen door. The colonel himself was an amiable-looking but very proud man of about forty. He was a college graduate, the only one in the entire town. Immediately upon being introduced, he seized on the opportunity to tell a stranger the story of his native land.

Cudjo (or Cudjoe) was a former Coramantee warrior who had been brought to Jamaica and sold as a slave, and who had incited a slave revolt in 1690. Cudjo's Maroons (as bands of runaway slaves were called) fought their way to the mountains in the western part of the island, eventually settling in the desolate, impenetrable section that we were in now. Here Cudjo established an independent state, whose capital he called Accompong (after his brother). Cudjo's band survived by hunting wild hogs, growing crops, and raiding nearby plantations for sugar and other essentials (to say nothing of female slaves, whom they recruited or carried off with regularity).

Despite sending regiment after regiment, even recruiting mercenaries among black freedmen and Mosquito Indians from Nicaragua, and burning and terrorizing outlying Maroon settlements, the British were unable to dislodge Cudjo from his stronghold. Fighting went on, incredibly, for almost fifty years. Finally, exhausted and fearing the uprising would spread to the rest of the island, the British authorities formally sued for peace. A treaty was signed in 1738 that gave the Maroons full autonomy over the area they held (now renamed Maroonland). That autonomy remained, in varying degrees, until independence in 1962. Even now, if a fugitive takes refuge in Maroonland, the Jamaican authorities must petition the governor of Maroonland for his or her return.

We spoke to the colonel for a few more minutes and even saw the treaty, an astonishing torn and weathered one-page document preserved in a kind of exaggerated BroDart. It was written in a flowing hand in the king's English, and underneath was Cudjo's mark. Then Smitty and I left and wandered across the green. A muffled chanting, regular and rhythmic, like a heartbeat, began to make itself heard.

"Dat from de cave," said Smitty, as the chanting got louder.

We walked nearer when suddenly Smitty put his hand on my arm. He had a grip like a vise. "Can't go no closer, mon. De spirits get you. Cudjo still in there."

We sat on the grass and listened. Neither of us spoke. I don't know how long we sat there, but when we finally got up, it was getting dark, and Smitty said it was time to try and make our way back to Montego Bay.

As it turned out, it was past time.

All the taxis had left, and no one, it seemed, who possessed any form of motorized transport was going to Montego Bay. Smitty rubbed his chin and pondered a bit.

"Maybe we go to Magotty and take de steamer."

"What's a steamer?"

"De steamer, mon," he repeated. "De railroad. Dere be a train due at about eight that go to Mo' Bay. We get a ride down de mountain, no pro-blem."

We did get a ride. It was in a vehicle that sometime in recent history had been a pickup truck. As guest of honor (meaning that it was my five dollars that we gave to the driver), I got to sit in the front.

A mere ninety minutes later, we arrived at the railroad station in Magotty. Smitty led the way as we walked into the waiting room. The second we were inside, I stopped and had to fight to keep my eyes from darting all over the place. The waiting room was lined with wooden benches along the walls, and the benches were packed—old men, women, children—with what seemed like a sea of dark brown faces staring at me, no one saying a word. There was no animosity in the stares, but they were stares all the same, and I was in the interior of Jamaica, and it was night. I realized suddenly how young black men feel wandering into a waiting room filled with white faces in Alabama, or New York, or anywhere in America for that matter.

Turning to leave seemed like a bad option, so I walked to the center of the room and sat cross-legged on the unfinished planking floor facing the large framed picture of Captain Morgan (the pirate) on the wall. I pulled out my Walkman, put on the headphones, and turned on the tape. Then I noticed a young guy, about twenty, standing across the way, holding a boom box, staring at me more intently than the rest. He walked across the room slowly, eyeing my Walkman.

He stopped where I was sitting and looked down. We stared at each other for a moment, then he pointed at the Walkman. I turned off the tape and took off the headphones.

"What you listenin' to, mon?" he asked

"Uh, the Go-Gos," I replied.

He nodded slowly.

"How about you?"

He mentioned some person or group's name that I didn't begin to understand. Then he paused, never taking his eyes off me. "Want to swap?" he asked.

For the next hour, I listened through my headphones to the best reggae I'd ever heard. I never did find out who it was. The rest of the room listened to the Go-Gos singing "We Got the Beat" and "Our Lips Are Sealed."

Finally, Smitty came by and tapped me on the shoulder. He looked nervous. "De steamer might not come tonight, mon. I got to get back to Mo' Bay."

From the look on his face, I could see that disappointing his employers by not showing up for work was not an option. "Can we get a taxi?" I asked.

Smitty nodded. "Gonna be ex-pen-sive, though."

What a surprise.

Smitty left me and went out to scour the town. He came back about twenty minutes later and said that he had found a taxi—a taxi in this case being a car that ran with a driver who was willing to do the round trip to Montego Bay. The driver wanted twenty-five dollars, a hefty sum to him perhaps, but not so bad when considered against the other option of sleeping on the floor of the waiting room.

We piled into a Chevy that had come off the line sometime

after World War II and took off. For the entire trip, the radio continuously played the song that was currently Number One on the Jamaican charts. The beat was rhythmic and intoxicating, and the lyrics consisted solely of the names of any number of hideous diseases that ended in "itis." So, for about forty minutes, I listened to endless repetitions of "el-eph-an-ti-tis, po-lio-my-e-li-tis, e-quine en-ceph-y-li-tis."

When we finally got back to Miranda Hill, I paid the driver and said goodnight to Smitty. As I walked back to my room, softly singing, "el-eph-an-ti-tis, po-lio-my-e-li-tis, e-quine en-ceph-y-li-tis," I stopped suddenly. I realized that something had happened, and I'm not sure quite how to describe it. Suffice to say that by the time I left Jamaica, I would not have been prepared to say that Cudjo *wasn't* in that cave.

Return to Massachusetts, April, 1995: The night of the purchase.

Immediately after dinner, one of us avoided helping with the dishes, cleverly eluded the awaiting garbage, and snuck off with *Cudjo's Cave,* almost giddy at the prospect of reading of ghostly raids in the night and the humbling of a great world power by an untutored military genius.

Hmmm. The first chapter was puzzling. There was no mention of Jamaica. Or Cudjo. Instead of Maroonland in the 1700s, this was Tennessee in 1861 and seemed to be about a white person, a Quaker named Penn Hapgood. Maybe Cudjo would come later, in a flashback or something.

But there never was a flashback. It took a while, but the truth finally set in. *Cudjo's Cave* had nothing to do with Cudjo. Not the Jamaican Cudjo, anyway. The Cudjo in *Cudjo's Cave* was indeed a runaway slave, but this Cudjo did not lead a revolt against the British or anyone else. This Cudjo was childlike and superstitious, with an ape's brow and arms that reached almost to the ground. He could barely grasp rudimentary language and lacked the skills to perform all but the crudest functions of survival. This Cudjo was gripped by terror when firelight caused shadows to dance on the walls of his cave.

And Cudjo was not the only broadly drawn character in the book. Whites seemed a tad caricaturish as well. Northerners, like Hapgood, were all virtuous and fine. Southerners were either drunken, uneducated, sadistic, leering, slaveless, and poor, or drunken, educated, sadistic, leering, slave-holding, and rich. They whipped, they burned, and they branded, all in graphic detail. They would have raped, too, but authors couldn't get away with that in 1864. The only thing missing was the twirling of the ends of mustaches, although that was probably in there somewhere.

And then there was Pomp, the freed slave. Pomp was tall, handsome, and fabulously built. He spoke English as if he had attended Cambridge. He had a knowledge of poetry, understood a smattering of Greek and Latin, and was a darn good fighter, doctor, and ethicist. Kind of a Paul Robeson for the 1860s.

In the end, Cudjo dies a hero's death, taking with him the cruel overseer from the plantation he had fled. Penn Hapgood nobly puts aside his pacifist beliefs and agrees to kill and maim in a good cause. The only slave-holding white portrayed as having any shred of decency whatever renounces his evil ways and shifts his allegiance to the Union. Pomp escapes to the North to join in the struggle.

It was a very confusing book. *Cudjo's Cave* had certainly been popular, or at least noteworthy, or it would not still be collected. Yet it was little more than a propaganda tract, almost burlesque, reminiscent of the movies made in Hollywood during World War II in which the Japanese were all cruel, deceitful fanatics, and myopic besides. Literary tastes certainly change, but, after all, *Cudjo's Cave* was written only twenty years before *Huckleberry Finn.*

Writing this poor engenders a certain natural curiosity, especially if it's still around over one hundred years later. Who was this Trowbridge anyway? Had he ever even been to Jamaica? Fortunately, in addition to the usual sources—BAL, the encyclopedia, and a number of dealers whom we pestered with regularity—there was an autobiography Trowbridge had written in 1903, and they had it (of course) in the Pequot Library.

John Townsend Trowbridge was born in a log cabin in Oneida County, New York, in 1827. Although he was descended from English gentry and was, by marriage, a distant relative of Richard Henry Dana, his branch of the family had run to hard times, and his father had been bound out to a farmer, John Townsend. Young John, his namesake, spent his boyhood helping his father raise sheep, although he found the time to immerse himself in the classics and teach himself to read French. When John was eighteen, the elder Trowbridge died, and John was sent to live with a married sister in Lockport, near Buffalo.

He won a local prize for poetry in 1845, and by 1847, after brief stints at farming and teaching school, he had moved to New York City to make his name as a writer. Although he enjoyed some success—he was paid twenty-five dollars for one of his stories—Trowbridge found New York too competitive and, fifteen months later, relocated to Boston.

Feeling himself "only a 'prentice hand," Trowbridge had taken to using the pseudonym Paul Creyton in New York and continued to do so in Boston. He intended to remain Creyton only until he produced "more mature compositions," but, as his popularity grew, Trowbridge was reluctant to eschew the commercial advantages of the nom de plume.

Of the sincerity of Trowbridge's abolitionist sentiments there can be little doubt. He was most impassioned on the subject. So impassioned, in fact, that one might ask why he did not, like millions of his fellows, volunteer to join the action personally. Yet, although he was thirty-three and in excellent health when the war broke out in 1861, he did not enlist. "I was eager to bear my own humble part in the momentous conflict," he noted, "and took up again the only weapon I had any skill to use." Perhaps, but when Trowbridge received offers from a number of periodicals to use that weapon in covering the war as a correspondent, he declined.

He chose instead to remain in Boston and build on the success of an earlier abolitionist novel, *Neighbor Jackwood.* His next effort would be "a partisan book, frankly designed to fire the Northern heart." Toward this end, he set the novel in Tennessee, a place he had never visited, and filled it with characters the likes of whom he had never met. Nonetheless, he must have been confident of the book's ultimate success because he abandoned Paul Creyton and wrote under his own name (thus accounting for "by the author of Neighbor Jackwood" on the spine).

The publishers must have been reasonably confident as well. They put off the January 1864 publication date "till a much larger edition than was first contemplated can be projected." In the interim, they mounted an advertising campaign that, even by today's lurid standards, would have to be described as determined. Trowbridge claimed to have been embarrassed:

> Pictures of the cave were on envelopes and posters . . . a bookseller's window (was) rendered attractive by a pile of the freshly bound volumes erected in the similitude of a cave. A private letter to the author from Secretary [of the Treasury Salmon P.] Chase, then at the zenith of his fame as a national financier, was made to service in ways he could not have anticipated. It was printed and extensively copied by the press and the interior of every street-car in Boston was placarded with a signed extract from it, outstaring the patient public week after week in a manner that would have made the great Secretary wince . . . as it did me.

Wincing or not, Trowbridge made gobs of money. When *Cudjo's Cave* was finally released in late February of 1864, it sold ten-thousand copies in three days. It had a number of almost immediate reprints, was imported to Europe within six weeks, and a British edition was published three years later. The initial popularity did not wane. *Cudjo's Cave* was in print for over thirty years, and, in 1890, it was dramatized in a three-act play entitled "Penn Hapgood or the Yankee Schoolmaster."

Whether or not he "fired the Northern heart" no one really knows. But while many northern hearts ceased to beat altogether on the bloody battlefields of the South, Trowbridge used the proceeds from *Cudjo's Cave* for a down payment on a big new house.

It was this house that was the indirect cause of Trowbridge actually visiting the region that had made his fortune. In August 1865 he was solicited to produce a "description of the principal battlefields and the condition of the States lately in rebellion." Initially, he was reluctant—after all, "the journey would undoubtedly be attended by hardships, discomforts, and some danger"—but this reluctance was soon overcome by the inducement of full expenses and sufficient remuneration to pay off the mortgage he had taken on the house as well as "adding a goodly sum to my bank account." So, Trowbridge agreed to visit all the battlefields that he had earlier avoided and wrote a book called *The Desolate South, 1865–1866: A Picture of the Battlefields of the Devastated Confederacy*. This book was also a success.

Upon his return, Trowbridge became an editor of *Our Young Folks,* a magazine for adolescents published by the owners of *The Atlantic*, for whom he had written before and during the war. *Our Young Folks* developed a large and devoted readership, and with contributors such as Charles Dickens, Louisa May Alcott, Harriet Beecher Stowe, and Henry Wadsworth Longfellow it is easy to see why. Trowbridge, in his own work, turned mostly to writing for boys, both publishing in magazines and creating a series featuring "Jack Hazard." He continued to prosper financially and was even able to take his family to Europe for three years, traveling across the Continent and staying at fine hotels. He died, ironically, on Lincoln's birthday in 1916. He was eighty-eight years old.

In a prolific career, *Cudjo's Cave* remains by far Trowbridge's best-known work. While the book lacks literary merit, it is not without historical value. Where there has been a good deal of debate as to whether or not Jim in *Huckleberry Finn* was drawn satirically, there can be no such question about Trowbridge's Cudjo. He, and the other blacks in *Cudjo's Cave* (with the almost ludicrous exception of Pomp), were portrayed as they were because Trowbridge thought his descriptions appropriate, and, unlike Harriet Beecher Stowe, who was sufficiently skilled on the page to keep her paternalism soft, Trowbridge let his attitudes come roaring on through. It is shocking to realize that even so fervent and dedicated an abolitionist—and he was most certainly that—saw blacks as childlike primitives. What's more, given the book's success, he was clearly not alone.

So, that left only one question. Did the title have *anything* to do with Jamaica? Had Trowbridge even heard of the heroic figure to whom he makes eponymous reference in the title, as brilliant a guerrilla leader and as important a freedom fighter as has ever existed?

Nope.

The allusion to the Jamaican Cudjo was completely accidental.

> The cave, the burning forest, the firelit waterfall came to me in two or three hours of concentrated thought. I adopted *Cave* at once as part of my title but felt it was necessary to make some felicitous addition. I was some time, indeed many nights and days, in finding a fit name for my runaway slave. *Cudjo* was finally decided upon and *Cudjo's Cave* for the book.

Oh, well.

Chapter 6

Outside the world of rare books, if the name Dr. Abraham Simon Wolf Rosenbach came up in conversation, most people would have no idea who he was but, if pressed, might easily conjure up the image of a Freudian psychiatrist, complete with couch, beard, and funny accent. Within the world of rare books, however, *everyone* has heard of A. S. W. Rosenbach. For book dealers in particular, Rosenbach is a legend. Even today, he is venerated as kind of a Babe Ruth, Henry Ford, and P. T. Barnum all rolled into one. What Dr. Rosenbach did to earn this reverence was to buy and particularly to sell rare books for more money than had ever previously been thought possible. When he stood up on April 3, 1928 at Sotheby's in London and bid £15,400 for the original manuscript of *Alice in Wonderland,* when even the rarest first editions of the work had never before sold for more than £500, the world of rare books changed forever. And, even though, as with many markets, the rare-book market crapped out during the Depression and has had its ups and downs since, every prestigious rare-book dealer of the 1990s who is so inclined owes his or her ability to charge outrageous prices for their books directly to Rosenbach's influence.

In addition to his commercial activities, Rosenbach was a scholar (his title a result of a Ph.D in English literature), a showman, and, after *Alice in Wonderland,* a celebrity. He was written up in the *New York Times* and had pieces on book collecting published in the *Saturday Evening Post.* He never married but, rather, had a series of illicit affairs, the longest and most public of which was with Carrie Price, a married woman whom he set up in her own lavish apartment and then, after she was free of her husband, refused to marry because she was not Jewish. He liked to sail his boat, read his books, tell dirty stories, eat fine foods, and drink a quart of whiskey a day, all of which he did until his liver gave out in 1952.

The house on DeLancey Place just south of Rittenhouse Square in central Philadelphia in which Rosenbach lived at the end of his life and which he shared with his brother, Phillip, an antique furniture dealer, has since been converted into the Rosenbach Museum. The museum is the repository of Phillip Rosenbach's staggering collection of antiques, including a number of pieces from the royal families of Europe, and A. S. W. Rosenbach's equally staggering collection of books and manuscripts. The latter has been supplemented by a number of other treasures that were acquired after A. S. W.'s death. Among these are Bram Stoker's original handwritten notes for *Dracula.* It was these notes that we had specifically come to Philadelphia to see.

We checked into the Latham, a nice prewar hotel on Rittenhouse Square with comfortable rooms at excellent prices, and then called to confirm our appointment with Elizabeth Fuller, the museum librarian. We were told she was going to be out until one-thirty, so in advance of our engagement, we decided to get into that old Rosenbach spirit by having an agreeable meal and a couple of drinks. Adhering to the oft-proven theory that people who know books like to eat, we asked for a restaurant recommendation, and the person on the telephone suggested Beaujolais, then a brand-new bistro on Twentieth Street, just up from DeLancey Place.

Beaujolais had red banquettes, black-and-white cane and bamboo chairs, and a tin roof painted over in silver and gold. Our waiter was in his early twenties with close cropped hair and a couple of days' carefully cultivated stubble on his face. He was tall and so thin that his cheekbones stuck out like crags, and when he turned around, his shirt looked as if it were on a hanger. As he recited the specials, he leaned forward and lowered his voice conspiratorially. It was like being served by an anarchist. When the food arrived he said, "That looks really good," in a way that strongly implied he was hungry.

He was correct, however—the food (linguini with seafood in a saffron and carmelized onion broth, and scallop, mussel, and vegetable chowder) *was* good, as was the wine, and there were little chocolates in the shape of red-foil lips with the check. And so, fortified for the afternoon, we left for our tour of the Rosenbach Museum.

The building itself was a three-story, red-brick double town house with a marble landing and a plaque in front that read, NATIONAL REGISTER OF HISTORIC PLACES. The front door was made of intricately wrought iron, and next to the door was a little sign that said, RING BELL FOR ENTRY.

Inside was a sumptuous entranceway with high ceilings, gold mirrors, and statues. When we had initially spoken with people at the museum, we had been informed that, at the Rosenbach, if you walk in anytime during business hours, even without an appointment, a volunteer would be available to take you on your own personal tour. When we arrived, on a cold Tuesday afternoon in January, there were no other visitors. As a result, when we entered the lobby, there facing us was a small semicircle of expensively dressed elderly women, eyeing us with what seemed to be eagerness. Immediately, two of them stepped forward to take our coats. It was like walking into a brothel specializing in women on Social Security.

Another woman, younger than those in the hall, stepped out of the door of the gift shop, which was to the left of the entrance, and said, "Hello, you must be the Goldstones." She gestured toward a woman at the left of the semicircle. "This is Thelma. She's one of our docents, and she'll take you on the tour." The other women looked disappointed. "When you get to the collection on the third floor, she'll hand you over to Elizabeth Fuller."

Thelma stepped forward. She was a short, thin, attractive woman in her seventies, carefully groomed, wearing a silk scarf and a tasteful black dress cut exactly at the knee. She held out her hand toward the room on the right.

"Won't you step into the parlor?" she asked, in a tone reminiscent of our daughter, Emily's, first-grade teacher telling the class to line up for recess.

The parlor was spacious, with a huge fireplace over which leaves and little Grecian figures on horseback were carved into the mantle. There were two large portraits on the back wall, one of Phillip and one of the doctor, and a painting of an incredibly beautiful woman on the side wall to the right. The ceilings were high, which was fortunate, because one of the antique chests was at least eight feet tall. We looked around. There were no books.

"Please have a seat," directed Thelma. "You can sit anywhere where there is a red cushion."

We sat in two chairs by the fireplace. Thelma arranged herself on a sofa across from us.

"This was the home of the Rosenbach brothers," she recited in a tone somewhere between practice and awe. "Dr. Abra-ham-Si-mon-Wolf-Rosen-bach was born in July 1876 and received his doctorate in 1901 in English literature from the University of Pennsylvania. Dr. Rosenbach was instrumental in forming many private libraries, including the Widener Library. He was known as the Napoleon of the auction house. He got the highest prices, and he paid the highest prices.

"He lived here at the end of his life with his older brother

Phillip. Phillip was a furniture dealer. He was the dandy—he had his tailor visit him two or three times a week. Across the street is Pearl S. Buck's house. Actually, the Rosenbach brothers lived most of their lives in a house a few doors down from here, but they took over this house in their later years because they could put in an elevator . . ."

Thelma went on for a bit, and it was all very interesting, and we wanted to be polite and all that, but, after driving three hours, then polishing off a large meal and several glasses of wine, we wanted to see some books.

Thelma was unmoved. The tour started in the parlor, and that was that. "See this?" she asked, gesturing toward the fireplace and a small, intricately woven needlework screen, with a swan in the center, stretched across a dark wood frame and mounted on an easel-like stand. "Can you guess what this was used for?"

"Uh . . ."

"Well, they used to put screens in front of the fireplace because, during the smallpox era, women used to fill their scars with wax, and the screen kept the wax from melting when they sat close to the fire." She turned and pointed to the portrait of the beautiful woman on the wall. "This is a picture of Rebecca Gratz painted by Thomas Sully. How old do you think she was when she sat for this?"

The woman in the portrait look to be about twenty, but it didn't take a whole lot to know that this was a trick question.

"Thirty? Thirty-five maybe?"

Thelma shook her head. "She was fifty." When we gawked, she added. "Now remember, this is a painting, not a photograph, but still Rebecca Gratz was so beautiful that when she met Sir Walter Scott, he was so taken with her that he used her as the model for Rebecca in *Ivanhoe*."

We sat in the parlor for over fifteen minutes. From there, we toured the dining room and the entranceway and peeked into the garden. We saw a jeweled serpentine necklace, gold bracelets stripped from ancient Egyptian princesses, and funeral eyeglasses from the Ptolemaic period, all purchased by Phillip. We saw another Thomas Sully painting, this one a huge landscape with a small girl on a beach. There were Edwardian Royal silver and Stueben glass, a marble console weighing in excess of one thousand pounds for which the dining room floor had to be reinforced, stained-glass windows depicting the muses, a couple of Egyptian sarcophagi in the garden, and various Greek and Roman statues on marble pedestals that used to stand in the Metropolitan Museum of Art.

On the entire first floor, however, there was not one single book.

"Where are the books?" we asked again. "When do we get to the books?"

"Don't worry," said Thelma, "we'll get to the books . . . now, over here is a really exquisite piece . . ."

"Well, what about . . ."

"NOW COME OVER HERE!" she said suddenly.

Dutifully and silently, we followed Thelma up a winding marble staircase. On the wall was a portrait of a Rosenbach ancestor who looked like Charles Durning dressed up as a Pilgrim. There was another portrait, a little farther up, this one of Rosenbach's mother, a formidable, glowering woman with thick black hair and eyebrows. We got to the second floor, and Thelma took us into a room done entirely in French period furniture. We saw a big clock that looked like a marble statue.

"Thelma. *Where are the books?"*

Thelma stopped, then dramatically threw open a door.

"*Here* are the books," she said.

They were in a tall, glass-fronted case. There were firsts of *Don Quixote* and at least twenty copies of *Robinson Crusoe.* There were forty-some volumes of Buffon's *Histoire Naturelle,* fully illustrated with animals and birds so lifelike they looked like they could growl or chirp. There was a wonderful collection of Defoe, at least one hundred volumes, as well as *Moby Dick,* Edgar Allan Poe, Christopher Morley, *Leaves of Grass,* Hawthorne, Holmes, and Emily Dickinson.

"Dr. Rosenbach thought you should have at least three copies of everything," Thelma informed us. "One to read, one to show, and one to lend. But this is only the study. Now," she said with a twinkle in her eye, "would you like to see his library?"

The library was on the third floor. Thelma took us up the stairs and knocked on a door. When it opened, she told a man of about thirty who we were, then immediately disappeared. It was like being handed off on the Underground Railroad. The man ushered us into a small, windowless office filled with boxes, file cabinets, and computer terminals and brought us over to a tall woman in her thirties with straight hair, who was wearing a green jacket adorned with a pin on which was incorporated a skyline photograph of, of all places, Cleveland.

"Hello," said the woman with a smile that did nothing to dispel her seriousness, "I'm Elizabeth Fuller."

The library was just down the hall. It was so large, it was divided in two, about a thousand square feet altogether, which, we realized, was larger than the one-bedroom apartment we had lived in for seven years in New York.

In the first room, the bookshelves ran all the way around in a big square, with only a little passageway left open leading to the second room. There were thousands of books, many in custom-designed clamshell boxes. There were original manuscripts and handwritten notes and books in parts the way they used to be published in England. You could literally spend a week there and not do everything justice.

Just under the ceiling, across the top of the bookcases, was a series of amazingly intricate reproductions of English country houses and cottages, sort of like dollhouses, only so detailed that they looked like they had been made with a magnifying glass. Some of them had little creeping green vines clinging to the sides.

"What are those?"

"Those were made especially for Dr. Rosenbach," said Elizabeth. "They are made entirely out of paper, even the vines. The man who did them originally constructed them as Christmas presents for his daughters. He did a new one each year. Dr. Rosenbach saw them and was so enchanted that he had some commissioned for his library."

She led us into the second room, which was also ringed with bookshelves. "This is the Americana room," she said. "Dr. Rosenbach was very interested in Americana."

We studied the books. A sample of the titles in the Americana room included:

Experiences of a Forty-Niner
Dodge City, the Cowboy Capital
The Public Papers of Governor Cleveland
The Burning of the Steam Boat Ben Sherrod
Goody Two Shoes
The Bay Psalm Book
The Indian Bible

There was a large wooden table in the center. On the table were some books and papers.

"You mentioned on the phone that you were interested in the *Dracula* notes," said Elizabeth. "So I took them out for you. Shall we look through them?"

Dracula is a phenomenon. Since its publication in 1897, an unimpressive first printing of three thousand copies in a shoddy, unattractive, dull yellow binding, it has never been out of print. It has been translated into dozens of languages and has sold millions of copies around the world. Filmmakers everywhere have made and remade the original story, and God knows how many uncredited spin-offs take the book as their inspiration. Stage productions on both Broadway and London's West End are mounted every decade or so. There are *Dracula* fan clubs and comic books.

As a result, one of those original three thousand, in any decent shape at all, even without a dust jacket, can now fetch well over $10,000. Even later printings of that first edition sell for over $5,000. But what emphasizes the collectibility of *Dracula* more than anything else is that reprints also command prices into the thousands. For example, we have seen the Grosset & Dunlap photoplay edition, issued to coincide with the release of the Bela Lugosi film and featuring a couple of publicity stills from the studio, sell for more than $2,000. Only this and *Frankenstein* of all the photoplay editions are worth anything at all, although a number of dealers, particularly those with a Hollywood clientele, are trying to push up the prices. Still, almost any photoplay other than these two can be had for under $100. And that number, until very recently, was $50.

Our own copy, another Grosset & Dunlap reprint, this time a reprint of an earlier reprint without publicity photos or any other Hollywood connection, cost us $200 after considerable wrangling with a dealer. The main selling point of this edition was the dust jacket, featuring an illustration of a woman lying in a trancelike state, stretched out on a bed, with a pair of huge eyes gazing at her through a window. As the little penciled-in price read $350, we were exceedingly pleased with ourselves over the purchase, although when we got home and had a chance to look more closely, we did notice another little penciled-in entry that read $50, which had been carefully erased.

But the real phenomenon of *Dracula* is not the book itself, but the incongruity between the work and the personality of the man who wrote it.

Bram (shortened from Abraham) Stoker was born in 1847 just north of Dublin. He was Protestant, what was euphemistically called Anglo-Irish, the third of seven children of a moderately well-to-do career civil servant. He was well on his way to following in his father's footsteps when, in his capacity as unpaid theater reviewer for the Dublin *Evening Mail,* he had a chance to meet the actor Henry Irving after a performance of *Hamlet.*

It was 1876, and Irving seemed to be just another of the many promising but little-known performers traveling from the London stage. But Henry Irving was not the same as those others. In addition to prodigious talent and an ego to match, Irving burned with ambition. Uneducated, from Cornwall, excluded from polite society, Irving was determined to raise the profession of acting to a level of respectability equal to that of doctors or lawyers. His scheme was to buy a major London theater so that he could choose and maintain creative control over every production.

In 1878, in pursuit of his vision, Irving bought the Lyceum Theatre in London. He was sufficiently savvy to know that in order to make this work, he was going to need someone who was willing to toil behind the scenes, faithfully and thanklessly, attending to all those crummy little details that are beneath the consideration of a genius. He immediately offered the job of business manager to Stoker.

Irving's decision to purchase the Lyceum turned out to be the most brilliant move in a brilliant career. It transformed him from a mere actor into an institution of Victorian society, the single most important and respected member of the English theater. He was even knighted in 1896, the first of his profession ever to be so honored.

Irving's choice of Stoker was inspired as well. Stoker counted up the receipts, kept the appointment book, wrote speeches, and accompanied the great man everywhere, checking out the accommodations and taking care of the luggage. He put up with temper tantrums, public slights, and constant condescension, without even one recorded instance of complaint. For twenty years after he took that job, Bram Stoker labored, and by all accounts labored happily, as—and there is no other way to say this—a professional ass-kisser.

But, being that it was Henry Irving's ass that he was kissing, Stoker got dragged along in the wake and became something of a minor celebrity himself. He got to meet Mark Twain and Walt Whitman, discussed the Irish question with Gladstone, and had dinner (along with Irving, of course) with the prince of Wales. Nonetheless, if you had told anyone in the 1890s that a hundred years later more people in the world would know Bram Stoker's name than Henry Irving's, they would have carted you off to the local insane asylum.

Somewhere around 1890, Stoker began taking notes for what was to end up as a six-year project originally entitled "Dead and the Undead," and culminate in the book we know today as *Dracula*.

There was nothing in Stoker's background to indicate that such a proper Victorian gentleman (he had once jumped off a bridge into the Thames to save a man from drowning) would choose such a subject or work so hard on a single book. He'd written before, but all of his previous efforts had been short stories or novels dashed off during odd hours and summer vacations.

With the very first look at the *Dracula* notes, however, it is plain to see that, for Bram Stoker, this book was going to be different.

"Now, here," said Elizabeth Fuller, holding up a sheet of paper laid in between plastic sleeves, "is perhaps the first outline for *Dracula*. You can see on the bottom that it was written on Lyceum Theater notepaper and dated in March of 1890."

We had to lean down to try and decipher Stoker's spidery handwriting. The letters were tiny—another incongruity as Stoker himself was a strapping athletic man, 6'2" tall.

The outline read:

Book I, "Styria to London" [Styria was later changed to Transylvania], *Book II, "Tragedy", Book III, "Discovery," and Book IV, "Punishment."* And bracketed next to each Book were precisely seven chapter headings. For example, for Book I there were:

Chap 1—The lawyers letters or
2—(Clerk visits Transylvania)
3—The Journey—Munich-blue flowers
4—arrival the Castle
5—Loveliness the kiss "this man belongs to me."
6—old Chapel curving earth sorts Virgiliame (notes in letter).
7—Dr. Sewards diary—fly—bound down

We continued to leaf through the notes. On every scrap of paper was some chapter or scene, laid out in the most minute detail. From his research, Stoker created a list of attributes that every good vampire should have, then carefully crossed out each one as he incorporated it into his character. Those items not crossed out never found their way into the novel. For example, his three-page memorandum to himself, entitled "Vampire," begins:

~~No looking glasses in count's house~~
~~Never can see him reflected in one—no shadow?~~
Lights arranged to give us shadow
~~Never eats nor drinks~~
~~Carries or led over threshhold~~
~~Enormous strength~~
~~Sees in the dark~~
~~Power of getting small or large~~
Money always old gold—traced to Salzburg banking house

And so it was throughout pages and pages of notes. He even had a page where he listed the characters, the heading of which read, "Dracula *Histoire Personae* Dracula." Among the characters who did not make it into the book were a detective named Cotford, a "psychic research agent," Alfred Singleton, and two servants to the count, a deaf-mute woman and a silent man.

"You may note the theatrical format of the notes," said Elizabeth. "It has been hypothesized, you know, that the character of Dracula is based on Henry Irving."

"How can that be? Didn't Stoker worship Irving? You don't base a four-hundred-year-old smelly ghoul who drinks blood on somebody you like."

"Perhaps," said Elizabeth.

"So what did Irving do? If it was true, then he must have had some idea that this tall thin guy with the big nose going around sucking the life out of all these people was supposed to be him."

"There was nothing documented," said Elizabeth, "but in those days, if you wanted to keep theatrical rights, you had to stage a performance, or at least a reading. They did such a reading at the Lyceum. It took place even before the book came out. Stoker asked Irving to read the Dracula part and Irving refused."

"Aha!" we said.

"Did you see this page?" she went on. "When Irving came to America, Stoker came with him, and I guess he wrote in his spare time. Here's his outline for chapter 26."

She passed across a sheet that contained a set of the usual detailed notes. But these notes were written on a piece of hotel stationery turned upside-down. The letterhead read:

CABLE ADDRESS, "BOLDT, PHILADELPHIA."
"THE STRATFORD,"
Broad and Walnut Streets

Geo. C. Boldt, prop'r

Philadelphia,. 189–

"Evidently he did some of the work for the novel about ten minutes from here," she said.

"The Stratford. Is that hotel still here?"

"The building is," said Elizabeth. "It merged with the Bellevue and became the Bellevue Stratford. You might have heard of that one."

"Legionnaire's disease, right? That's where it first happened. At an American Legion convention at the hotel. All those people got sick and died."

"Yes. They just call it the Bellevue now."

"Sound marketing decision." We leafed through some more.

"Is this a map?"

"That's very interesting," said Elizabeth. "This was done at Whitby. Stoker used to spend vacations there with his family. Do you remember in the book when the boat carrying Dracula, the *Demeter,* runs aground and the people of the town go onboard and find all the crew dead? And then a big dog runs off and heads for the graveyard? Well, that actually happened—not the part about Dracula, of course—but, like so many of the details in *Dracula,* the shipwreck was taken from real life. Even the part about the dog. In October 1885, a ship called the *Dimitry* ran aground, and we know that Stoker went to the library to read the local news accounts of the accident and then sketched the steep staircase that went up from the harbor. See, here it says, 'View from above.' Look how careful he was about accuracy . . ."

The heading on the page read, *"At Whitby the sun rises E.S.E."* Further down, it read:

> *When ship ran into Collier's pole. big dog jumped off bow and ran over pier—up Kiln yard & church steps & into churchyard.*
>
> --
>
> *local dog found ripped open & graves torn up*

As before, each of these entries was crossed out, meaning that Stoker used them in the story.

"Something else happened at Whitby," Elizabeth went on, "something that may have had a major influence on Stoker's plans for *Dracula.* Do you know George du Maurier?"

"Sure. He wrote *Trilby.*"

Trilby, published in 1894, three years before *Dracula,* was another phenomenon of the book world. But, unlike *Dracula,* which started out small and ended up big, *Trilby* began as a huge, unvarnished Victorian mega-hit—it broke sales records in Britain and sold over 200,000 copies in America at the inflated price of $1.75, and people all over Europe and America wore little "Trilby" hats with feathers in them—but within ten years it had all but disappeared from the public consciousness.

Trilby is the story of a young free-spirited artist's model living on her own in Paris. She poses nude, smokes and swears, sleeps around in an unconcerned fashion, and is adored by three British art students, but especially by Little Billee, who asks her to marry him and makes sketches of her feet.

Into this idyllic world enters a tall, thin, demonic Eastern European music teacher with hypnotic powers. Even worse, he is a Jew. Under his spell, Trilby abandons Little Billee and, although she is tone-deaf, becomes a world-famous opera singer. The portrait of a beautiful young woman living by her own rules was intoxicating to Victorian readers, and the idea of her being forced to perform against her will, even if it was only singing, turned out to be irresistible. Not surprisingly, the book stirred intense controversy, but the more polite society and the clergy denounced *Trilby,* the more it sold.

Today, although not one person in a hundred remembers *Trilby,* the character of the hypnotic music teacher still survives, and his name, Svengali, has become a fixture in the language.

"Well, as you may know," said Elizabeth, "du Maurier . . ."

"Was he any relation to Daphne?"

"Grandfather. In any event, du Maurier, like Stoker, was not primarily a writer. He was the cartoonist for *Punch.* He had even put Stoker and his family in one of his cartoons a couple of years earlier. They met one day in the summer of 1890, when both were on holiday. There is no record of what they discussed, but as Stoker was in the formative stages of *Dracula* and du Maurier was apparently toying around with *Trilby*—he had originally offered the idea to

Henry James, who was a good friend of his, but James had told du Maurier to write it himself—it is quite possible that they discussed each other's ideas."

"You mean Stoker ripped du Maurier off? Based the Dracula character on Svengali?"

"There is no record of that, but Stoker could not have helped but be aware of the tremendous success of *Trilby* while he was writing *Dracula.* In fact, *Trilby* was so popular and brought du Maurier so much unwanted celebrity that, when he died in 1896, it was widely assumed at the time that the book had killed him."

"What do you mean? Did the book rise up in the night?"

Elizabeth looked at us. "Evidently du Maurier was a very private man, and he was so beseiged by fans of the novel that he descended into depression and died."

"He died because he was a celebrity? It's hard to imagine that happening today."

"Just the reverse," said Elizabeth. She leafed through the pile, then took out a newspaper clipping. "You might find this amusing," she said. "It came out the year before *Dracula* was published."

It was a full-page article from the *New York World,* dated February 4, 1896.

VAMPIRES IN NEW ENGLAND
Dead Bodies Dug Up and
Their Hearts Burned to
Prevent Disease

Recent ethnological research has disclosed something very extraordinary in Rhode Island. It appears that the ancient vampire superstition still survives in that State, and within the last few years many people have been digging up the dead bodies of relatives for the purpose of burning their hearts.

"Near Newport scores of such exhumations have been made, the purpose being to prevent the dead from preying upon the living. The belief entertained is that a person who has died

> of consumption is likely to rise from the grave at night and suck the blood of surviving members of his or her family, thus dooming them to a similar fate."

"They dug up the bodies of dead relatives and burned their hearts?"

"Yes," said Elizabeth. "Newport has always been popular with the best families."

When we finished with the *Dracula* notes, Elizabeth took out a clamshell case that held a copy of the first edition of the book itself.

"This is one of the best copies still available," she said as we gingerly opened the cover of a book that was even flimsier, more brittle, and, frankly, uglier than we had imagined. The dust jacket seemed as if it could be reduced to dust at a touch. All the same, this book was a rare and obviously fragile piece of history, and there was something magical about being so close to it.

When we were done with *Dracula,* Elizabeth carefully packed up all the material.

"Would you like to see some other items?" she asked.

She went to the shelves and took out James Joyce's original, handwritten manuscript of *Ulysses*. Joyce had a weird vision disorder, so as he moved down a page the left-hand margin got progressively larger so that the writing appeared as an inverted right triangle.

"How these notes came to be here is very revealing of Dr. Rosenbach's style," said Elizabeth. He purchased these notes from Joyce's representative for nineteen hundred dollars. At almost the same time, he purchased a Conrad manuscript for three thousand dollars. Joyce was furious when he found out that Dr. Rosenbach had paid more for Conrad's manuscript than for his, and he demanded the *Ulysses* manuscript back. 'Okay,' said Dr. Rosenbach, 'you can have it back . . . for three thousand dollars.' Joyce couldn't come up with the money, so the manuscript stayed here."

After *Ulysses,* she showed us the *Bay Psalm Book,* which was the first book printed in America, and which is even rarer than the Gutenberg Bible. For almost an hour, she kept going back to the shelves and returning with treasures. She seemed perfectly willing to continue on indefinitely, but we were finally forced to ask her to stop on grounds of exhaustion.

"Thank you, Elizabeth," we said. "This has been great. Could we ask you something, though?"

"Sure."

"Well, you know that we're writing a book. What if a member of the general public wanted to see these books and notes—not someone in academia, or the press, or whatever, just someone off the street—if someone like that wanted to talk to you and see what we've seen, what would it take?"

Elizabeth looked at us. "An appointment and a photo ID," she said.

"That's it?"

"That's it."

Elizabeth led us back down the stairs. On the second floor, she paused.

"You did see the exhibit, didn't you?"

Before we could stop ourselves, we answered. "No." Oops.

"Oh, you must. It's excellent. It's an Americana exhibit, about the relationship between Native Americans and Europeans in pre-Colonial and Colonial times. Almost everything in the exhibit is from Dr. Rosenbach's collection."

We wavered. The ground floor looked so good. "All right." We followed her into two adjoining rooms on the left, which somehow Thelma had skipped.

"Not only is this exhibit unusual," said Elizabeth, moving right along, "but the site is unusual as well." She paused in the first of the two rooms. It was filled with display cases and exhibits mounted along the walls. "This was Phillip Rosenbach's dressing room." Then she gestured into the second of the rooms. "And this was his bathroom."

We looked around. "Is this really a bathroom?" The room could have slept eight.

"Oh, yes. See that case there? It's mounted on top of the bathtub."

So it was. The top that had been placed across Phillip's bathtub was large enough to hold a case housing three separate documents, the commentary for each, as well as a number of artifacts on the side. Apparently, when Phillip Rosenbach took a bath, Phillip Rosenbach took a bath.

The title of the exhibit was "Words & Deeds: Natives, Europeans, and Writing in Eastern North America, 1500 –1850." It dealt with the mutual influence of the cultures of Native Americans and the European settlers.

Once again, the exhibit turned out to be so fascinating that we wished we had seen it three hours earlier when we were fresh.

It began with the European point of view. There was a poster by a London merchant picturing a galleon and advertising fruits planted in Virginia, which was intended to lure settlers to the colonies. Nearby was a document by Marc Lescarbot, a French lawyer, describing Native Americans as sociable and generous, followed by an excerpt from John Smith's *The Generall Historie of Virginia, New-England, and the Summer Isles,* describing the Massacre of 1622 and calling the Indians "Bloody" and "barbarous," a "perfidious and inhumane people." There was a striking, amazingly detailed map, drawn in 1655 by a Dutch cartographer, showing the Atlantic coastline from Chesapeake Bay north to what is now Maine, with an entry for each of the known settlements and depictions of the different sorts of wildlife prevalent in each area. There was a sonnet by Thomas Morton in which he compares the New World to a "faire virgin, longing to be sped / and meete her lover in a Nuptiall bed," her lover being the European colonists, of course.

But what was really unusual about the exhibit was the insights into the Native American point of view. Even though current, revisionist history grants a degree of dignity and intelligence to peoples once thought childlike, survival of words such as *wampum* still portrays a society that was so hopelessly naive that beads were used as money. In fact, we learned at this exhibit that *wampum* had a much more complex meaning in Native American culture:

> No utterance at any diplomatic occasion was valid until authenticated by the exchange of wampum in the form of strings or belts. Acceptance of the gift of wampum was tantamount to acceptance of its message. In this way, wampum functioned like a certificate. Wampum also served to engender further diplomatic contact; its presentation was a gesture that required a reciprocal effort on the part of the recipient. The amount and color of the shell-beads reflected the importance and content of the message, which was memorized by the speaker, for whom the belt or string functioned as a mnemonic aid.

Also in the exhibit were documents and treaties and petitions; artifacts; a Bible translated into an Indian Language; a primer for Indian children to learn English; and captivity accounts, the first best-sellers to be produced on the continent. These included a pamphlet entitled "A Narrative of the captivity Sufferings and Removes of MRS. MARY ROWLANDSON, who was taken Prisoner by the INDIANS with several others and treated in the most barbarous and cruel Manner by those wild Savages: With many other remarkable Events during her TRAVELS, Written by her own Hand, for her private Use, and now made public at the earnest Desire of some Friends, and for the Benefit of the afflicted," complete with a woodcut on the cover showing hatchet-bearing savages charging toward the musket-toting Mary.

But most significantly, the exhibit brought home what must have been the bewilderment of a people used to what was substantially a nomadic, communal existence, suddenly coming up against a culture in which wealth is based on acquisition, particularly of land. The equally baffling concepts of purchase and sale and rent were exemplified by these two documents, which were hung side by side over Phillip's bathtub. The first, written by a Mohawk chief, read:

Brother Onas: [*Onas* was the Native American word for "quill" in this case it was used as a pun to refer to William "Penn," then governor of Pennsylvania.]

> *What we are now going to say is a Matter of great Moment, which we desire you to remember as long as the Sun and Moon Lasts, we are willing to sell you this Large Tract of Land for your people to live upon, but we desire this may be considered as part of our Agreement that when [we] are all Dead and gone, Your Grand-Children may not say to our Grand-Children, that your Forefathers [sold this] Land to our Forefathers, and therefore begone off them . . . Let us all be as Brethren as well after as before our giving you Deeds for Land, After we have Sold our Land, we in a little time have nothing to shew for it, but it is not so with you, Your Grand-Children will get something from it as long as the World Stands, our Grand-Children will have no Advantage from it. They will say we were Fools for selling so much Land for so small a Matter, and curse us, therefore let it be a part of this present Agreement, that we shall treat one another as Brethren to the latest Generation, even after we shall not have left a Foot of Land.*

The second document came from the Onondaga chief Canasatego, and was written in 1744. It read simply:

> *Our brother* ONAS, *a great while ago came to Albany, to buy the* Susquehannah *Lands of us; but our Brother the Governor of*

> *New-York . . . advised us not to sell him any Land . . . and pretending to be our good Friend, he advised us, in order to prevent* Onas, *or any other Persons imposing upon us . . . to put it into his Hands; and told us, he wou'd keep it for our Use, and never open his Hands, but keep them close shut, and not part with any of it, but at our Request.*
>
> *Accordingly, we trusted him, and put our Land into his Hands, and charged him to keep it safe for our Use; But some Time after, he went away to* England, *and carried our Land with him, and there sold it to our Brother* Onas, *for a large Sum of Money . . .*"

On our way out, we stopped by the gift shop. We had been at the museum so long that it was now closing, and we just had time to grab a catalog of the Dracula exhibit and one for "Words & Deeds." We have learned that regardless of how interesting we may find an exhibit or how intently we study it while we are there, it is difficult to acquire more than a superficial appreciation of the subject. Catalogs, which in addition to narrative text, often reproduce many of the documents, not only provide posterity to the event but can be insightful history in their own right. In this case, we learned more about each of these subjects from the catalogs than we had learned previously in all our other research, in school, or by reading biographies.

For example, some weeks after our visit to the Rosenbach, we were leafing through the introduction to the "Words & Deeds" catalog when we found this:

> *Indians placed great value upon live testimony and personal experience. To them, written texts hopelessly lacked the vital power of the spoken word. For example, while the Seneca chief Red Jacket acknowledged the need for a cadre of literate Indians to guard against fraudulent treaties, he deemed writing a culturally inappropriate medium for Indian expression. He chided whites for trying to remake Indians in their own image and mocked what appeared*

to him to be a central component of Euro-Americans' sense of superiority. "You say there is but one way to worship and serve the Great Spirit," he said. "If there is but one religion; why do you white people differ so much about it? Why not all agreed, as you can all read the book?"

Chapter 7

One day in early March 1998, we received a telephone call from Maggie Griffin of Partners & Crime.

"How would you guys like to sit at our table at the Edgars?" she asked.

The Edgars are the Edgar Allan Poe Awards, sponsored by the Mystery Writers of America (MWA), generally considered the most prestigious of any award given in what is perhaps the most popular genre in all fiction. This year, for the fifty-third annual awards, the event was being held at the Sheraton New York. Cocktails were from six to seven in the Royal Ballroom, followed by the dinner and the awards ceremony in the Imperial Ballroom, after which there was to be dancing to a live orchestra. Dress, Maggie told us, was black-tie, and the subsequent invitation read "Dress To Kill," although it did note "black-tie optional." Tickets were $70.

With visions of Oscar night and of rubbing elbows with the likes of Sue Grafton, Robert B. Parker, Elmore Leonard, Patricia Cornwell, or John Le Carré, we immediately accepted. When we hung up the telephone, each of us had the same question.

"Why do they want us?"

So, before they could change their minds and invite somebody better, we mailed Maggie $140 and began to pore through our clothes closets for the appropriate thing to wear. In one case, not a single dress or pair of shoes was even remotely suitable, and, in the other, the tuxedo was in serious need of seam relief. The evening had already begun to have serious expense potential, but so what? This was to be our first glitzy awards dinner at a fancy New York hotel. When we told our friends and relatives, they were intensely envious, even though we had to tell most of them what the Edgars were.

The next step was to do some research and, most importantly, to read each of the books nominated for Best Mystery Novel, the big prize of the evening.

The five nominees certainly covered a wide territory. *Cimarron Rose* by James Lee Burke was a gritty, tightly spun thriller set in a small, nightmarish Texas town with more than its share of homicidal maniacs; *Dreaming of the Bones* by Deborah Crombie was a literate, atmospheric Victorian whodunit with numerous references to the Bloomsbury circle; *A Wasteland of Strangers* by Bill Pronzini was an allegorical novel about the arrival of a Christlike figure in a small town, which ignites prejudice and hatred and provokes a killing; *Black and Blue* by Ian Rankin was the bleak tale of a copycat serial killer in Scotland, based on the exploits of a real-life serial killer of the 1970s who makes a fictional appearance in the book; and *The Purification Ceremony* by Mark T. Sullivan was a "Ten Little Indians" series of gruesome killings of the members of a hunting party, one of whom has a Native American alter ego who matches wits with the killer.

The favorites were said to be Burke and Pronzini, skilled and graceful writers, both of whom had been nominated many times before but had yet to win. Our own straw poll of mystery-book store employees, however, indicated that *Black and Blue* was the best book. Personally, we were rooting for Pronzini, because he had the only book in which the presence of a murder seemed incidental to higher literary aspirations.

The Edgars, we had been told, has been gathering prestige in recent years, with the winner for Best Mystery Novel getting a definite bounce at the sales counter. And there is clear interest in this prize from a collector's point of view. Book*Line* reported that firsts of *Cimarron Rose* and *Black and Blue* were already going for $100 or more.

But much more importantly, the Edgars are a unique opportunity for the industry to showcase its best. Despite the huge success of the Le Carrés, the Cornwells, and the Graftons, most mystery writers, even those with established track records or up-and-comers like Charles Todd, receive only modest advances and limited print runs, and almost no recognition outside the genre. For example, when we read the list of nominees to both sets of our parents, they claimed to have vaguely heard of *Cimarron Rose,* although they had no idea who James Lee Burke was and seemed to think he was Larry McMurtry, and had not heard of the other four at all. It is the collective dream of this industry to extend the popularity of the superstars to a wider range of mystery writers. And what better opportunity to acquaint the public with your product than a glamorous black-tie awards dinner?

We sought out every bit of information we could find. Book*Line* pointed out that a firsthand account of last year's event could be found in a magazine called *The Armchair Detective.*

The Armchair Detective is a sort of *Bon Appetit* for the homicide set. The story on the Edgars was written by Laurie R. King, a former winner herself, who had chaired the committee that chose the Best First Mystery Novel the year before—thus explaining who *she* was. (All the awards are chosen by committees consisting exclusively of MWA members.) The article came complete with pictures, including one prominent one of Diane Plumley of Murder Ink in a cocktail dress with her hair up. The article itself was entitled "Diary of an Edgar," and went through what King went through month by month, leading up to the awards. What we were really interested in was the dinner itself, so we skipped through the trials and tribulations of picking the winner until we got to it.

"After champagne [oh, goody, we thought], we all dive out into the crush, to be claimed by our respective agents and editors. The Edgars banquet is a big, posh affair attended by writers, publishers, agents, and you name it. A highly edible meal is served with ruthless efficiency to several hundred men and women, most of whom are either table-hoppers too busy or nominees too nervous to eat."

And so, after several weeks of puzzlement, Laurie R. King had finally revealed to us our place in the Edgar hierarchy: we were the You Name It.

At some point we had decided, oh what the hell, let's do it right and stay over in Manhattan. After all, who wants to drive home at maybe two in the morning, after hours of champagne and dancing, only to have to get up at six-thirty to rouse an intensely crabby six-year-old who thinks *she* didn't get enough sleep? So we begged Emily's friend's parents to take her for a sleepover and then, when the big day arrived, drove into New York.

We got there around noon, parked in front of the Sheraton, and waited while the doorman busily unloaded a staggering number of giant suitcases for an entire Japanese family that had pulled up in a van. Even when he was done, however, although he could see that we were waiting, he made no move in our direction. Finally, after apparently determining that there were no other high rollers present, he accepted our car keys and the $5 that by then we were displaying prominently with our car keys. He handed us a ticket and walked away, so we unloaded our own bags, then walked through the front door into the lobby. We noticed immediately that it was filled with people wearing name tags, and, although we couldn't read the names, we could see that they were all from places like Turkey or Sri Lanka.

We checked in. The room we had reserved ordinarily cost over $300, but we had gotten the special Mystery Writers of America rate of $220. There was no special rate on the valet parking, however, which was $30, an outrageous sum even for midtown Manhattan. Still, we were in high spirits, peering around the lobby, trying to figure out which of the people milling about might be famous mystery writers.

Once again, no one offered to help us with our bags, so we went up to our room, 1919. There was a king-size bed that covered two-thirds of the floor space, a chest of drawers upon which sat a huge TV, a desk, and the usual bare hotel amenities. Even though the room was perfectly clean, it looked dirty. The paint was cracked, the tiles in the bathroom had separated, the furniture was old and cheap, and the walls were so thin that when the couple next door flushed their toilet, it sounded like Niagara Falls. (You could hear their conversation very clearly, too. He wanted to do it. She didn't.)

We went downstairs and checked the electronic board for the schedule. There were a number of other events being held on the same day as the Edgars, including a convention of British employees of Ford Motor Company and an estate-planning council. Occupying the Imperial Ballroom for the afternoon was an International Aortic Surgery Symposium. When we went up to the mezzanine to check it out, we realized that all those people we had seen in the lobby from Third World countries were, in fact, cardiovascular surgeons. On four television screens just outside the ballroom, in full view of passersby, they were running a video of open-heart surgery. Someone was sticking a bunch of little pins with sutures into an exposed area of someone else's still-beating heart.

Down the hall, the last group of our coconventioneers for the day had put up a big sign:

GENDER AND DEPRESSION:
Perspectives for the New Millennium
(This program is endorsed by the National Depressive and Manic Depressive Association)

At about five o'clock, after the cardiovascular surgeons had finished with their presentation of Cerebral Metabolic Suppression During Hypothermic Circulatory Arrest, we checked out the mezzanine once more and noticed that the MWA had started setting up and that there was a stack of seating charts, complete with a list of all the attendees for the awards. We grabbed one and shot back up to 1919 to check it out.

First, we looked for our own names. Phew. There we were, Lawrence and Nancy Goldstone, table twenty-seven, the Partners & Crime table. Most, but not all, of the tables were labeled. Murder Ink had two tables, as did Black Orchid, and the Mysterious Book Shop had three. Avon Books was there, HarperCollins, Henry Holt, Viking/Penguin, William Morrow, Doubleday—all the major publishers, including St. Martin's, our publisher, had taken tables. So had *Reader's Digest, Ellery Queen's Mystery Magazine, New Mystery Magazine,* and the Agatha Christie Society. There were representatives from film and television. *Law & Order* and *The Practice,* both of which were up for Best Mystery Episode in a Television Series, were at tables two and thirty-six, respectively, and the A&E Network, which had been nominated under Best Television Feature or Mini-Series, was at table fifty-seven. *L.A. Confidential, Donnie Brasco,* and *Conspiracy Theory* had all been nominated for Best Mystery Motion Picture, so we looked for a big Hollywood star—the previous year Sam Waterston had attended; we'd seen his picture in *The Armchair Detective.* But there was no one on the list. No Johnny Depp, no Kim Basinger. Sigh.

Then we started looking for the names of all the big-time mystery writers. Sue Grafton wasn't there. Patricia Cornwell wasn't there. Robert B. Parker wasn't there. John Le Carré wasn't there.

Walter Mosley wasn't there. Carl Hiaasen wasn't there. Elmore Leonard wasn't there. Lawrence Block, who was nominated for Best Short Story, wasn't there. Even Bill Pronzini, whom we were rooting for, wasn't there. Unlike the Oscars, where cameras pan the crowd and all sorts of actors and directors and screenwriters who hadn't received nominations that year show up both as a testament to the event and as a means of supporting their industry, almost no significant mystery writer who was not a nominee was going to be present. Of those who might be considered industry stars, only Mary Higgins Clark, Michael Crichton (who had flown in from Los Angeles, but only, as we found out later, to support his friend, the Japanese publisher Hiroshi Hayakawa, who was being honored for a lifetime achievement in publishing), and Nelson De Mille had opted to attend.

At ten after six, not wanting to be too early or too late, we went downstairs. There was already a crowd swirling in the hallway between the Royal Ballroom, where cocktails were being served, and the Imperial Ballroom, which would open at seven for dinner, and where the Sheraton staff was feverishly setting up. Long tables had been arranged in the hallway, on which were piled stacks and stacks of paperback and audio books. These were apparently there for the taking, as were copies of a special edition of *AB Bookman's Weekly* and *New Mystery Magazine*. Some of the guests, obviously veterans, had brought along shopping bags in order to more conveniently stash their haul.

We got our name tags and walked into the cocktail party. We were struck by the casual dress of a large number of the attendees. Usually, when an invitation reads "Black-Tie Optional," it means that the few who are *really* unwilling to wear a tuxedo can opt for a dark suit.

But here, only about half of the men were wearing tuxedos, and of those who were not, most had made no attempt at formality whatever. There were a number of sports jackets and even some turtlenecks. There was one man in a ponytail sitting at a table who was wearing only a black shirt, black pants, and tennis sneakers. The women, by and large, had dressed up more. There was even a sprinkling of real evening gowns, including one knockout Scarlett O'Hara red-velvet number.

The lack of universal formal dress gave us a twinge, but we passed it off. Mystery people, as we had come to know, are unusual, to say the least, and the mood at the cocktail party, as Laurie R. King had predicted, was boisterous. We each grabbed a glass of white wine (no champagne was yet visible), and walked around watching people meet, greet, hug, and assure each other of success later on. Occasionally we said hello to people we knew, but for them this was business, and they moved quickly past us to work the room. A television camera was busy trailing around Hiroshi Hayakawa and his family, which we found out later was for Japanese television. This seemed to be the only media present, although we did have our photo snapped by Diane Plumley's husband.

"I did this last year and sold the pictures to *The Armchair Detective*," he told us.

Very soon a waiter went around with a set of chimes, indicating it was time to move across the hall for dinner. When people didn't move quickly enough, they dimmed the lights.

On our way into the dining room, we overheard the following conversation:

Man: What table are we at?

Woman: Fifty-three.

Man: Fifty-three! What are we doing at fifty-three!

Woman: It doesn't matter. We could be right next to somebody important.

We moved inside, looking around. The live orchestra, which consisted of about ten oblivious white-haired gents, was playing a swing number, so we stole a dance before we sought out our table.

We had only had a glass of wine apiece at the cocktail party, because we still hadn't seen any champagne, and we assumed it was going to be a long night, with a lot of wine at dinner.

This turned out to be a serious blunder.

Actually, fifty-three was a great table, right next to the dance floor, opposite the podium. Twenty-seven, on the other hand, was all the way on the side, next to the wall.

No matter. We plunked down and introduced ourselves to the other members of the Partners & Crime table. We said hi to Maggie Griffin, who was wearing long, dangling earrings with little skulls on the bottom.

"By the way," we said, "where's Bill Pronzini? How come he isn't here?"

"I don't know," answered the woman next to us. "Jim Burke wasn't going to be here either. You know, he doesn't fly and all that. It's hard for him to get here." She paused. "But then they made a phone call."

"You think they called to tell him he had won?"

She shrugged and turned to her Caesar salad.

Despite what Laurie R. King had written, there was no table-hopping during dinner. There wasn't time. The chicken with fruit sauce was there before the last piece of romaine had been speared.

Strangely, there were no wine glasses at the table when we sat down, although there was a wine list. Brian, Maggie's boyfriend, ordered three bottles for the table. There were ten of us. He seemed to hand the waiter something when he ordered. When the bottles came, the waiter gave Brian a credit-card receipt to sign.

"You have to pay for wine?" we asked, visions of a wild, champagne-filled evening receding rapidly.

Everyone tried to chip in, but Brian refused gallantly. "I've been coming here for years," he said, "and someone has always paid for it. This year is my turn."

Oh God, we thought, three bottles of wine at Sheraton prices.

Filled wine glasses livened up the conversation immediately. We discovered that one of Brian's and Maggie's passions was taxidermy. There is a lot about taxidermy that is not obvious to the layman.

"I like to buy old, beat-up pieces and then spruce them up with new eyeballs and new tongues," said Brian. "You can get them in catalogs. And you know, cats' mouths especially shrivel up after awhile, so you inject them with a relaxer and then restuff their lips to make them puffy again."

The remains of the dinner were swept away, dessert was plunked down on the table, and the awards began. Feeling bad about the nonfree wine, we had once again had only one glass each.

For the next two hours, we were pinned to our chairs. There were sixteen awards altogether, which comes out to two awards every fifteen minutes. Allowing about two to three minutes for each acceptance speech, that left over five minutes for each MWA presenter to discuss how hard it was to pick the winner, how hard it was to select the nominees, and how hard it was to get in touch with publishers and persuade them to submit any books at all.

A surprising number of those who came to the podium to speak or to present awards were older women. This is not the image one generally associates with books about sex-crazed serial killers and dismemberment. And then, instead of reading from a teleprompter, they often held up sheets of paper, adjusted their glasses, complained about the lighting, and proceeded to mispronounce the nominees' names.

The first award was for Best Children's Mystery Book. Barbara Brooks Wallace won for *Sparrows in the Scullery*. Ms. Wallace was not available, so her statuette was accepted by her editor.

"Thank you very much," said the editor. "Barbara would have loved to have been here, but she broke her wrist." The editor paused. "And you all know how hard it is to write with a broken wrist—"

"So we're going to drop her," said someone at our table.

As we moved through the categories—Best Mystery Play, Best Critical/Biographical Work, the Robert L. Fish Memorial Award, Best Mystery Episode in a Television Series—there was a curious lack of interest in the room, and, in some cases, an almost incredible level of rudeness. At the Viking/Penguin table, right next to us, which had no one nominated for anything, they were making openly derisive comments and laughing during the presentations. Although *they* had about five bottles of wine at *their* table, they all wore the expression of people who had lost the lottery in the office pool and had been forced to attend the dinner against their will. By the time the last award for Best Mystery Novel was given, every one of them had gone home except for one woman who was sitting in her raincoat ready to bolt out at the first opportunity.

This was all too bad because the acceptance speeches were often lovely. Many of the awards went to people who were either first-time authors or in areas of the business like original paperback, where winning made a big difference to their immediate future, and the excitement they evidenced was real and very touching. Hiroshi Hayakawa, who had brought his entire family from Japan, spoke at length about the publishing house founded by his father almost on the day World War II ended, which was dedicated to bringing the best of Western literature to the Japanese reader. Barbara Mertz, who writes under the pen names of Elizabeth Peters and Barbara Michaels, and who won the Grand Master Award, was witty and intelligent.

Lawrence Block did win for Best Short Story. His friend Harlan Coben came to the podium to accept the award.

"Larry couldn't be here tonight," he said. "He's on a cruise ship somewhere in the Indian Ocean. Before he left, he gave me some notes. They've been sitting dormant in my wallet for some time . . . reminds me of my adolescence. Larry said that he was thinking of saying that he'd rather be here than where he is, but that would require too great a suspension of disbelief."

Perhaps the most interesting contest of the evening was that for Best First Mystery Novel by an American Author, the next-to-last award. This is an extremely important award, more so perhaps even than Best Mystery Novel. Best First Mystery is generally won by a young author who has received a tiny advance and an even-smaller first printing. The award is, if not a guarantee, at least an assurance of a bigger pop for his or her next book. This is the award to which collectors pay close attention, for it is here that the next *"A" Is for Alibi,* or the next *Postmortem* will be found.

This year, among the five nominees, two were of particular note. They could not have been more dissimilar.

23 Shades of Black by K. j. a. Wishnia was begun ten years ago in the mountains of Ecuador on an electric typewriter. It featured Filomena Buscarsela, an Ecuadorian immigrant, now a New York City policewoman. It was everything a first mystery should be—hard-boiled, gritty, passionate, and raw. It was far from a perfect book, but nonetheless held you by the sheer force of its protagonist's voice. K. j. a (actually Ken) Wishnia, after at least four rewrites and dozens and dozens of rejections by agents and editors, finally self-published *23 Shades of Black* as a paperback, using the imprint "Imaginary Press." It received virtually no notice in the mainstream media. Imaginary Press, even after the success of *23 Shades of Black,* was still in the red.

"It got to the point," Wishnia said, "that a thousand dollars here or there didn't matter. I just had to get the book out there."

After publication, but before his nomination, Wishnia was signed by Dutton for a three-book deal. We asked him how it felt to be nominated.

"Are you kidding? It's like playing sandlot stickball and having the Yankees pull up in a big car and say 'Hey kid, ever hear of the World Series? Well, we want you to play in it.' "

Los Alamos, on the other hand, was written by Joseph Kanon, formerly head of trade fiction and then publisher at Houghton-Mifflin. Without offering the manuscript for general submission,

Binky Urban of ICM, Kanon's high-powered mega-agent, gave the book to John Sterling, head of the then-new Broadway Books. Sterling was a former Houghton-Mifflin editor-in-chief and Kanon subordinate, and gave Kanon what the *New York Times* reported as a half-million-dollar advance, a figure Broadway Books would not confirm but did not deny.

Los Alamos was slick, polished, and professional. It reeked of Big Money Book. It was reviewed everywhere, generally with enormous enthusiasm, was heavily advertised, and had a first printing of about fifty thousand books according to Book*Line.*

We were sitting about ten feet from Ken Wishnia as the time for the award approached. Wishnia appeared to be in his early thirties, slender and boyish looking. He was sitting between his wife, Mercy (who is Ecuadorian and the reason he was in the mountains ten years ago) and his new editor, Audrey LaFehr. He was wearing a gray rumpled sports jacket and a narrow tie. He seemed to stop breathing as the presenter read through the nominees. LaFehr's hand was on his back.

Then, the winner was . . . Joe Kanon.

Kanon strode to the podium amid polite applause and a standing ovation from the Broadway Books table. He stood for a moment, surveying a crowd that doubtless included any number of writers whose work Houghton-Mifflin had summarily rejected over the years, and proceeded to give an acceptance speech in which he said, among other things, "But I suppose if you're willing to keep reading them, I'll keep writing them, and maybe I can do better next time." He did everything but look down at his shoes.

"Yuck," said a woman at our table.

After Kanon returned to his seat, Elizabeth James came to the podium to present the award for Best Mystery Novel. The winner was James Lee Burke.

Amid a general standing ovation, Burke walked to the podium quietly, with genuine shyness. He stood up in front of his peers, looked at the award, and said simply, "This is probably the happiest night of my life." There was no doubt whatsoever that he meant it.

Then, after Burke had returned to his seat, the proceedings were adjourned. It was time for the dancing.

Immediately, the same group of white-haired men who had been playing when we walked in returned to their places in the orchestra, except this time, instead of Benny Goodman, they began to play, at superhigh volume, such notable octogenarian favorites as "La Bamba," "I Want To Hold Your Hand," and "(I Can't Get No) Satisfaction." By the time the first chorus of "La Bamba" had been reached, the room had become virtually deserted.

The only people who stayed to dance those one or two dances were us, Ken and Mercy Wishnia, and Audrey LaFehr. Around us, the Sheraton staff had already rushed in to begin to break down the room.

After "Satisfaction," we took the hint and left. We wandered down to the lobby just in time to see the last 1.5 seconds of game four of the N.Y.-Miami NBA playoff series, in which 6' 5" 260-lb. Larry Johnson of the Knicks and 6' 10" 275-lb. Alonzo Mourning of the Heat threw lots of punches at each other, while the Knicks coach, 5' 9" 160-lb. Jeff Van Gundy, hung on to Mourning's leg like a malignant terrier.

The following day, although the fight received extensive coverage in both the newspapers and on television, we saw not a single word devoted to the most celebrated awards given in mystery and detective fiction. In fact, in the days that followed, there was no mention at all of the Edgar Awards. It took fully a week before some of the winners' tombstones appeared in the *Times*.

After we checked out of the Sheraton, we carried our bags through the door to the garage, where we had been told to pay for parking separately. When we gave the ticket to the attendant, he said, "Forty dollah."

"Forty dollars? They told us thirty when we checked in."

"Thirty plus five-dollah tax and five-dollah valet charge."

"What's the five-dollar valet charge?"

"Five dollah. You had the doorman park you car."

When we got back home, still grumbling about nonfree wine and the five-dollar valet charge, we decided to call one of the booksellers we knew (not someone from our table) to talk about the Edgars. We asked why everyone had been in such a hurry to leave.

"What did you expect? Didn't you see how boring it was?"

"But why?" we asked. "Why didn't anyone show up? Where was Sue Grafton, for instance? Or Patricia Cornwell? What about Robert B. Parker?"

"Oh, they never come."

"You mean in all these years, the top writers haven't come to the awards?"

"Well, some do. Elmore Leonard has come a lot. Dick Francis comes when he's in the country. Walter Mosley comes every year. Mary Higgins Clark is wonderful. But the others . . . they reach a point where they don't come anymore. They're too big to come. They don't need it. There's the politics, too. Not everyone joins the MWA. There's one writer who should have won about five years ago, and everybody knew it, but they gave it to a member instead."

"Someone told us that James Lee Burke wasn't going to come until they called him."

"You mean, told him he was going to win? I don't believe that. I believe that the winners are kept secret. When Otto Penzler used to chair the panel, he didn't even tell his wife."

We spoke to this same bookseller again, about two months later.

"You remember when you asked about winners being told in advance? I'm appalled. I found out that it might have been true."

Chapter 8

In April 1997, a month before the publication of *Used and Rare,* our editor sent us a Xerox of David Streitfeld's March 9 "Book Report," a column that appears regularly on the last page of the weekly *Washington Post Book World.* She had stuck a little yellow Post-it on the top, on which she had written, "The first mention!"

It was the exclamation point that got us. We read eagerly, impatient to see the words of praise heaped on *Used and Rare* by such an eminent authority as Mr. Streitfeld.

> Late next month [he wrote], St. Martin's Press will publish *Used and Rare* a leisurely description of the way people bought secondhand and antiquarian books in the old days before, say, 1996 . . .
>
> By the end, the couple have acquired no more than a very basic knowledge; if *Used and Rare* were a cookbook, it would tell you how to boil eggs and steam vegetables. It's a pleasant tale, however, and especially noteworthy because it's probably going to be the last of its kind. The Goldstones tramp around to all these stores and dealers and

> specialist shops in person; if they had started now, instead of a mere four years ago, much of their acquiring would be done over the Internet.

Everyone is entitled to their opinion, of course, regardless of how desperately they reach for metaphors, but in the last sentence of this paragraph, at least about us, Mr. Streitfeld is simply wrong. In fact, had we been restricted to the Internet, we probably would never have become interested in rare books and first editions at all.

He goes on to assert that while he doubts on-line book buying will ever "do more than supplement going to the physical stores" for the purchase of *new* books, for used and antiquarian books, "collectors will need a computer. If they aren't on-line, they can't play the game."

There is no doubt that the Internet is a powerful new force in book dealing. And the issue, as Mr. Streitfeld correctly points out, will inevitably be whether on-line book buying will replace the physical act of going to a bookstore or merely serve as a supplement to seeing, touching, and experiencing books, even those that you do not ultimately buy.

For the used- and rare-book buyer, the Internet currently means search and purchase services that combine the listings of thousands of dealers from all over the world. This, in turn, allows the collector to browse by title, author, or subject, with subpasses for price (above or below a certain amount), edition, and in some cases condition. The major services are Bibliofind (bibliofind.com), Interloc (daniel.interloc.com), Advanced Book Exchange (abebook.com), and, for higher-end books, Bibliocity (bibliocity.com) There is even a new search engine, mxbookfinder (mxbf.com), that merely combines all the others (except Bibliofind) in one master list for easier, one-stop shopping. At the time of this writing, the huge on-line booksellers for in-print books, like amazon.com and barnesandnoble.com, had yet to make the full leap into the out-of-print market, but that will probably have changed by the time this is read.

So, for example, if you're looking for *Used and Rare* but have forgotten the title (just a hypothetical, of course—who could forget *Used and Rare*?) you can log on to, say, Bibliofind, and enter "Goldstone" under author. You will then get back a list of over fifty books, virtually everything written by someone named Goldstone, among which will be *Used and Rare.* Other books by Goldstone include the definitive *John Steinbeck Bibliography* by Adrian Goldstone and John Payne, *The Tears of Rangitoto* by Robert Goldstone, *Revolution and Rebellion in the Early Modern World* by Jack A. Goldstone, *History Preserved, A Guide to New York City Landmarks and Historic Districts* by Harmon Goldstone, *Thornton Wilder, An Intimate Portrait* by Richard Goldstone, and *Run Far, Run Fast* by Lawrence Goldstone, although not this one, since it was written in 1937. The more narrowly you define the criteria of your search, of course, the less volume you have to wade through in the results.

Along with telling you which dealers *may* have the book you are interested in (updating is an ongoing problem), each entry will generally include condition (although these terms—fine, near fine—are as subjective as ever), edition, whether there is a dust jacket, whether the copy is signed, sometimes a few laudatory comments by the dealer, and, of course, the price. When these services first got started, the price disparities among dealers selling the same book in purportedly the same condition could be so enormous as to be laughable (although probably not to the dealer on the high end). As the services matured, however, prices tended to, if not equalize, at least gravitate toward the same universe.

If you decide to actually purchase the book, you may then click on that entry, and the dealer's order page will come up, letting you know who they are in detail, where they are located, the payment terms that they will accept (almost always a credit card), any additional costs, such as shipping, and what their return policy may be. *Once you place your order, you are then doing business with the dealer, not the search service.* If you get stiffed, you've got to fight it out with the dealer on your own—a circumstance of some significance, especially if the dealer happens to be located in someplace like Germany or Libya. The search services are very explicit in disowning any responsibility for your transaction. In the case of ABE or Bibliocity, it wouldn't matter much anyway, since ABE itself is based in Vancouver, British Columbia, and Bibliocity in Brisbane, Australia.

Despite the sophisticated, far-flung feel of all this, the search services, like most Internet businesses, began (and in most cases continue) as mom-and-pop operations. We witnessed the beginnings of one of them in the spring of 1996, when we visited Farshaw's, a bookshop in Great Barrington, Massachusetts.

Farshaw's is a small shop on Railroad Street owned by Michael and Helen Selzer. We had known Michael and Helen for three years, ever since our very first tentative forays into the used-book world.

"Oh hi, Larry and Nancy," said Helen somewhat breathlessly when we walked in the door. She was dressed, as usual, in black. She gestured to us excitedly. "Come look. You might want to put this in your book."

We walked over and saw that what she was gesturing at was a new computer that was sitting on the desk behind the counter. We thought it must be for accounting since, up until then, Farshaw's had used little waitress pads to generate invoices.

"We're starting a new business," she announced triumphantly.

That in itself was not a surprise. The Selzers always seemed to be involved in one new venture or another. They stocked not only their own books but leased shelf space to a number of other area dealers as well. In addition to the shop, they owned Selzer & Selzer Antiquarian Books and Berkshire Book Auctions. Michael had gotten involved in placing private papers of prominent persons with libraries around the nation and was something of an archivist in his own right. The Selzers were, without question, the most entrepreneurial people we had ever encountered in the book business.

Helen led us over to the computer. "Wait till you see what

we're doing. This is terrific," she said. She sat down and keyed in an entry. We watched with interest. Up until then, Helen had always seemed to us like a low-tech kind of a person.

A screen came up. It read, "Bibliofind."

"There it is," announced Helen.

"What's Bibliofind?"

"It's a computer service. Anyone will be able to go on-line and buy a book from any dealer in the country."

"You've got every dealer in the country on that?"

"Oh no. Just about one hundred-fifty so far. But this is the future of bookselling. Every dealer is going to sign up eventually."

We nodded. At the time, our own knowledge of the Internet was restricted to the incomprehensible instructions, replete with terms such as *World Wide Web, chat rooms,* and *FAQs,* that we regularly received on Prodigy, the on-line service we had decided to try in order to see how much money we were losing each day in the stock market. The idea that this would be the future of the atavistic world of book collecting seemed, to say the least, far-fetched.

"Did it cost you a lot to set this up?" we asked finally, hoping Michael and Helen hadn't just happened on that one idea too many.

"A lot less than you'd think," Helen replied. "The technology was surprisingly simple. Michael did it."

Michael was Oxford educated and fabulously intelligent and had an encyclopedic knowledge of well, almost everything, although up until then we hadn't thought that had included computer science.

Helen clasped her hands in front of her and eyed us like a Jewish grandmother offering up a third helping of gefilte fish. "Don't you want to try it?"

"Sure."

"Great," she said, pulling her chair up close to the machine. She pointed at the screen. "One of the things people don't like about on-line services is all the time it takes for a screen to come up." This was true. When we logged on to Prodigy, even with our brand-new, state-of-the-art, 9600 bps modem, our screen seemed to come up in sections, a line here, part of a picture there, seemingly at random. "That's because of the graphics," Helen explained. "They're the slowest to upload."

We both noticed that Helen's language had taken on a distinct technological flavor. She hit a couple of keys and almost instantly a search form came up.

"We use almost no graphics," she said. "We figure that our customers want speed, not a pretty layout."

"If we try this at home, will it come up this fast?" we asked.

"No, not quite," she said. "We have immediate access to the database. You may have to wait a few minutes . . . but not nearly as long as if we had graphics."

Right.

"So," said Helen, looking at us expectantly, "tell me a book you've been looking for, and I'll show you how this works."

"Uh, what about *Mrs. Bridge*?" This was in our pre-Kemet days.

"Great!" In the "Title" box, Helen typed in "Mrs. Bridge." "That was by . . ."

"Connell," we replied.

"Right." She typed in "Connell" in the "Author" box. "Now watch," she said. She hit the Enter key and we waited. A couple of seconds later, the screen came back:

"0 Matches for Connell, Mrs. Bridge. Another Search?"

"That means we don't have it," said Helen. "Try something else."

"Okay. What about *The Treasure of the Sierra Madre*?"

Helen made the appropriate entry, and once again after a few seconds, we got the "0 Matches" reply. We stood there and tried five different books (including some of our own) but didn't make a single score.

"Well," said Helen, not the least bit embarrassed, "when we have more dealers, we'll be able to get big lists for everything."

"And then you can sell the whole package to a big company and make a million dollars," we said jokingly.

Helen took a big breath and rolled her eyes. "From your lips to God's ears," she said.

We left Helen at the terminal, browsed about Farshaw's a bit, bought a few books, then went on our way. After we were outside, we looked at one another.

"That is the dumbest fucking thing I have ever seen in my entire life."

"Larry, do they really think people are going to use a computer to buy books they've never seen from a dealer they've never heard of and give him a credit-card number to boot?"

"And that's assuming that they can get any books."

For the next year or so, every time we went to a book fair, we saw Michael Selzer. Not as an exhibitor, though. Michael, a roundish, bearded, professorial type, would be walking jovially through the room, clad in a black T-shirt that read "Bibliofind" on front and back, chatting up dealers, trying to persuade them to sign up for his service. At Mariab, where he did rent a booth, instead of books he brought a computer terminal.

When we got home after Mariab, we logged on to America On-Line, our new computer service, and, out of curiosity, finally checked out the Bibliofind site. Once again, we typed in "Mrs. Bridge." We had by this time purchased the book, of course (twice), but *Mrs. Bridge* was the best test case. Again, there was a wait while the machine did whatever it did to get us the information.

This time, we got back five different entries.

Just one year after that, in 1998, Bibliofind boasted two thousand dealers and 6 million books in its database and was running weekly ads in the *New York Times Book Review.*

It occurred to us after this that our unerring ability to predict the future, as exhibited in the case of Bibliofind, was possibly the reason that we never made any money in the stock market.

While the search services may be the most convenient way for a dealer to make his or her inventory available to collectors, any dealer who so chooses (and most have) can go on-line individually, whether he or she subscribes to a service or not. Most dealers have combined both approaches and include a reference to their own home page on their dealer page of a search service.

In retrospect, it is easy to see why the Internet, and especially search services like Bibliofind, are so appealing to dealers. The Internet means immediate access to a super mailing list. For virtually nothing, certainly far less than it costs to produce and mail a catalog, a dealer can put his or her entire inventory on a screen. The result may well be an inquiry or an order from someone the dealer has never heard of before, perhaps someone who lives in another country altogether, a customer the dealer could never have hoped to access in the old ordinary course of business.

And a home page can be every bit as inventive, funny, and inviting as a catalog cover. Here, for example, is what happens when you call up Biblioctopus, a high-end dealer based in Century City, California:

BIBLIOCTOPUS
The Masters of Low Tech
List 47
First editions of the classics of fiction
and a splash of non-fiction
interspersed with a surfeit of modern wannabes
some of which may someday make it
and even some of the once thought weighty
pathetically hanging on by their fingernails
the whole addended with the incidental
and vaguely associated
(48 B.C.–1995)

If your interest has been piqued (and whose wouldn't be?), you can then browse through much of their catalog. And there is no doubt that, in the future, almost every dealer will have his or her entire catalog, at least in summary, on-line.

The Internet saves wear and tear on the notoriously fragile dealer psyche, too. A dealer doesn't even have to *talk* to the customer, just answer E-mail, which most consider a giant plus. We were in a shop, as a matter of fact, where, when the phone rang, the dealer responded to whoever was on the other end with: "Are you referring to an E-mail inquiry? We will be E-mailing you back," and then, without saying another word, hung up.

Since all it takes to become a book dealer on the Internet is a home page, a computer, a modest outlay to get everything up and running, and hopefully a few books, a whole new group of "dealers" is springing up, and some of the older, more established dealers are considering ditching their shops altogether to save money. After all, it costs a substantial, sometimes prohibitive, sum to keep up a store. In addition to the rent, there's upkeep, utilities, insurance, taxes, and salaries, all of which become needless expenses when one is operating in cyberspace.

If, for the dealer, the Internet means access to a super mailing list, for the collector it is access to a super catalog—a simple and convenient way to locate a specific title, compare prices, and get some idea of condition, all without ever having to lift one's behind off whatever seat in which it happens to be planted. Even if you do intend to go to a shop to purchase a book, the search services can provide some terrific prepurchase research. It's nice to be able to say, "One-hundred dollars seems a little high for that. I just saw it on the Internet for sixty-five."

Although the exponential growth of the search services is an extremely recent phenomenon, certainly by the geologic rare-book standard, there were those who saw the potential of technology long before the Internet was a glimmer in the Defense Department's eye.

"ABE [Advanced Book Exchange] was the first on the Internet, but Interloc is the oldest service," said Dick Weatherford, Interloc's founder. "I began talking about this in 1982. You know, lecturing at seminars or going to Denver [the site of a yearly rare-book conference]. I tried to get people to see the role that computers could play in the out-of-print book business."

Weatherford was himself an antiquarian book dealer for twenty years before his Interloc days. He was also a college professor. What he had in mind was not a consumer-based service, but rather a dealer-to-dealer matching service.

"Finally in March 1994, I started up. This was in the days when there were no commercial enterprises on the Internet, as amazing as that seems now, so I started as a dedicated, dial-up 800 service, a private network for dealers. We had about twelve-hundred dealers, and we handled about fifty-thousand matches a day."

But things got bigger faster, and within two years Interloc was on the Web, now with eighteen hundred dealers and handling up to 150,000 matches a day. Even now, when its database is available to any collector who cares to log on, its primary focus is still dealer-to-dealer business.

"We're the only service that has date screening," Weatherford noted. "When a subscriber first puts up a want [a title they are trying to acquire for a customer or for stock], the system screens the entire database. If they check a second time, though, they will only see what has been listed since their last inquiry. No one else does that. We have subscribers with a quarter of a million wants. They don't want to see the entire database every time they log on."

Weatherford soon plans to take the business to the next level.

"We're going to redesign everything," he said. "I want to eliminate the dealer-to-customer direct link. Most of the dealers are reputable, but you'll always have your share who don't ship promptly or who misrepresent the condition of their books. What I'm going to do is to become a clearing house . . . the dealer will ship the book to me, and I'll examine it before I send it on to the customer. The dealer will only get paid if the book is in the condition it is said to be."

"That's very ambitious," we said. "It sounds pretty expensive, too."

"When did I say I didn't have money?" asked Richard Weatherford.

"Well, in our experience, people who have money didn't make it by providing services they weren't paid for."

"Well, what I plan to do is ask the dealers to give me the standard twenty-percent dealer discount, and I'll use that twenty percent to finance the clearing house."

Richard Weatherford's vision notwithstanding, the real next generation of on-line book selling in the out-of-print market may turn out to be something else entirely. The success of the on-line search services has attracted the attention of two very different groups of book (and computer) enthusiasts.

"I just turned twenty-one last week," Anirvan Chatterjee, creator, owner, and only employee of mxbookfinder E-mailed us (what else?) when we asked about his service. Mxbf was the service that combined the listings of all the other on-line booksellers.

"I graduated from U.C. Berkeley last month. I'm a programmer, a lifelong reader, and a fan of on-line bookstores," his message went on, "so my interest in building a shopping agent for on-line books was apparent. The site started off as a final project for a graduate seminar on Internet agents I was taking in fall 1996, but I kept working on the software afterward. I spent last summer interning with Microsoft."

"Is it true," we asked in our E-mail, "that you don't make any money on the sales or charge to display the list?"

"We don't charge any of the services we list for being included," came back the answer. "The primary goal is to bring the best selection of listings to our audience, and charging for entrance is incompatible with that."

"If there's anything else you want to pass along," we suggested, "please feel free."

"I got an A on the project," Anirvan Chatterjee replied.

At the other end of the spectrum from the whiz kid programmer, hardly old enough to vote, who does this for free or, at worst, for a good grade, is the looming Terminator-like presence of those who have caused the death of more independent bookstores than television—the Chains.

It started innocently enough. Amazon.com, faced with a growing number of requests for books that were not available from the publisher or the major distributors, like Ingram or Baker & Taylor, began posting wants with used-book dealers in order to satisfy its customers' requests. This must have been profitable because, soon thereafter, in early 1998, Barnes & Noble's president, Steve Riggio, made a deal with Richard and Vivian Pura, the owners of Advanced Book Exchange, to make the ABE database available to B&N's online subsidiary, BarnesandNoble.com. This was the first formal arrangement between the in-print and out-of-print cyber-services. Others, it is generally believed in the book world, are sure to follow.

When asked why b&n.com decided to strike the deal with ABE, Tom Simon, b&n.com's vice-president for content development, said that used books were "part of the picture," and it was an effort to make "the whole picture" available to their customers.

Michael Selzer had a drastically different view. When he heard about the deal, he fired off an E-mail to all the ABE subscribers, one of whom passed it along to us. In the E-mail, he stated (we're summarizing here; Michael is not terse):

1. *The sole goal of Barnes & Noble in making the ABE deal was to establish a presence in the out-of-print market in order to ultimately drive independent dealers out of business.*

2. *Barnes & Noble is currently stockpiling used books (250,000 as of this writing) and developing in-house manuals, training courses, and seminars to prepare for its invasion of the out-of-print market. In addition, they*

are running ads reading, "Barnes & Noble needs your good books."

3. Seven Barnes & Noble superstores have already established antiquarian departments on a test basis.

4. Bibliofind, before the ABE deal, had been approached twice by Barnes & Noble with the same offer but had turned them down.

5. He, Michael Selzer, had offered to raise money so that Richard Pura could buy ABE out of its contractual obligations with Barnes & Noble but was not given the courtesy of a reply by Mr. Pura.

The letter received mixed reviews from the dealers, many of whom were torn between the fear of losing their businesses to a voracious Barnes & Noble and a desire for the vastly greater exposure that a benign Barnes & Noble might provide.

"Michael Selzer is simply wrong," said Tom Simon. "First of all, I was working on this before I ever came to Barnes and Noble. Secondly, we don't own any percentage of ABE. We are not, to my knowledge, stockpiling used books. It is true that a few of our stores have begun collecting departments, but that has been a store-by-store decision and in each case was approved by a regional manager.

"There have been more Elvis sightings in our stores," he added, "than there are rare-book dealers."

It is impossible to know who is telling the truth. Tom Simon declined specifically to discuss the economics of either the deal with ABE or those of any markup b&n.com may place on used books. Still, the labor-intensiveness of the out-of-print book business seems to mitigate against the chains taking over entirely. We know dealers who travel for hours to go through collections of hundreds of books, all in order to find one or two that are worth buying for their shops. Unlike a new book, where an Amazon or a Barnes & Noble can offer deep discounts because they are buying by the thousands from publishers all too willing to sell at discounts themselves, every used or antiquarian book is essentially a one-of-a-kind item. Will the chains really want to take over a part of the industry where discounting, their number-one weapon, and the one largely credited with driving independent new-book stores out of business, is inapplicable?

For example, we were told (although not by Amazon) that amazon.com has a standard mark-up of 20 percent on the books that it acquires from used-book dealers.

"I don't see them doing all that work for only twenty percent," said Kevin Rita, one time when we were in West Hartford, "although personally, I enjoy dealing with Amazon. I've always found them to be well run and completely professional. They know what they're ordering, they don't waste my time, and I always get a check within a week."

"Twenty percent seems low to me, too," said Mike Polasko, the owner of the West Hartford Book Shop, an outstanding used-book store, positively stuffed with bargains, just down the road. Mike was loitering, as he often is, in Kevin's shop. Sometimes Kevin loiters in Mike's shop. We loiter in both.

"In fact," Mike went on, "a sporting-books dealer I know had a permanent want posted for a book called *Painting Nature's Quiet Places* by Thomas Aquinas Daly. The book isn't that valuable, but you almost never see it. He'd had the want up for months, maybe longer. Anyway, one day it comes up . . . on Interloc, I think. It's some dealer in Kansas, or maybe Montana, and the book is about seventeen bucks. He tries to get it, but it's already gone. The next day Amazon E-mails him and tells him, guess what, they've found *Painting Nature's Quiet Places*. Then they give him the price. Ninety bucks."

"That's the thing about the people who buy used books from Amazon or Barnes and Noble," said Kevin. "Most of them don't seem to be aware that there are search engines for used books at all."

That is likely to change. It seems clear that there will soon be more and jazzier access to used, rare, and antiquarian books on the Internet, complete, in this era of 50K+bps modems, with lots of graphics. And, if the consumer is lucky, the increased knowledge that comes with increased information will serve not only to make books more available to more people, but to keep prices under control as well.

So, with such a convenient and powerful tool at the collector's disposal—and one that promises to become a good deal more convenient and powerful—isn't David Streitfeld correct after all? Why would anyone in their right mind waste their time "tramping around to all these stores and dealers and specialist shops in person"?

Here's why.

It was during our Philadelphia trip. We had come mainly to see the Rosenbach Museum, of course, but whenever we go somewhere, we find out in advance if there are any bookstores that look worth visiting. So, just before we left, we made a quick check of the ABAA Directory on the Internet (we never said it didn't have its uses) and noted, among about five or six other entries, George S. MacManus Rare Books. Even then, we might well have passed this shop by in favor of the better-known Baumann's if not for a startling coincidence.

On the web page, right under the name "George S. MacManus Company," it read, "Clarence Wolf, President."

"Hello? Is this Clarence Wolf?"

"Yes," said a cautious male voice on the other end of the telephone.

"My name is Nancy Goldstone . . ."

"Yes?"

"This may sound strange, but do you have any relatives in Chicago?"

"Oh, you mean the Clarence Wolf from Chicago . . . no, I'm not related."

"Oh, I just thought . . . well, Clarence is such an odd . . . uh, uncommon name. I mean, there are lots of Wolfs but . . ."

"Yes," said Clarence, "I'm the only white male in America under fifty that I know named Clarence. How do you know the other Clarence?"

"He was my grandfather. He died last month."

"Oh, I'm terribly sorry."

"Well, it could have been worse, I suppose. He made it until just before his ninety-eighth birthday, and up until a week before he died, he was still dressing in a suit and tie every day and sitting down to read Churchill. Anyway, we're going to be in Philadelphia in a few days. Could we come by and see your shop?"

"Of course. We're on Irving Street," he said. "Do you know where that is?"

"Oh, that's all right. Larry's got a map. He can find anything."

"Where the hell is Irving Street?"

It was a windy mid-January day, and we were wandering the streets of central Philadelphia. We had asked at least four or five people who appeared to be genuine Philadelphians, including a man who worked for the bus company, where Irving Street was, but nobody had heard of it.

"It's supposed to be between Spruce and Locust, isn't it?"

Just then we looked up, and there was a facade stretching out over the street that read, "BOOKS" vertically.

"Oh, that must be it."

We put our heads down and cut through the wind to the shop. When we got there, however, it was immediately clear that this was not George S. MacManus Company but a store that sold medical books. We were cold, so we went in anyway.

A small, sallow woman with chopped, muddy red hair was being waited on at the counter by a tall, fleshy man with a ponytail. At the very back of the store were two desks, each occupied. The red-haired woman was buying three institutional-size paperbacks on obstetrics and gynecology. We waited until she finished her transaction.

"That will be one hundred and thirty-eight dollars and forty-nine cents," said the man with the ponytail.

Boy, did we pick the wrong field of writing.

He turned to us. "May I help you?" he asked.

"Yes. Do you know where the George S. MacManus Company is?"

The man with the ponytail shook his head no, but the woman at one of the back desks said, "Oh, they want to get to Clarence Wolf's shop. Mr. Foster may know." She then turned to the man at the desk next to hers and said in a louder voice, "MR. FOSTER, THESE PEOPLE ARE LOOKING FOR CLARENCE WOLF."

Mr. Foster slowly lifted his chin off his chest and looked up. He was a white-haired man in a blue suit with a cardigan underneath, and appeared to be about 150 years old. "Yesss," he said, looking vaguely in our direction. "Do you know Philadelphia?"

"No," we said.

"Are you going to drive there?"

"No, we're going to walk."

"Ohhh," he said, shaking his head infinitesimally. "It's a very long walk."

We didn't absolutely trust Mr. Foster's perspective on what might constitute a very long walk, but replied that we would take it into consideration.

"Make a right out of the shop, and go across Broad Street until you get to Juniper. Take a right on Juniper, and go half a block down, and you'll get to Irving Street. Take a left, and he's in the middle of the block. Maybe you should write that down."

"No, I think we can remember."

We thanked him, and as we were leaving the shop, we heard a little voice from the back repeating, "It's a verrry long walk . . ."

It took three minutes. Irving Street was actually a glorified alley only one block long. We'd probably passed it three or four times without noticing. The bookshop was the only storefront on the street. Everything else was the back of one of the buildings that faced out on the real streets.

Just as we arrived at the door, a gate was being pulled shut from inside. A man of about forty with a mustache and wearing a gray-down vest saw us and pulled the gate back, just far enough to allow him to reach the doorknob and crack open the door.

"Sorry, we close at five," he said.

Ordinarily in a situation like this we would consider begging, but it was clear from the man's face and tone that the 5:00 closing time was nonnegotiable.

"Well, what time do you open in the morning?"

"At nine," he said, and shut the door.

Try having that much fun on the Internet.

We decided that we did not have to stand for getting a door slammed in our faces, even if the shop was closed, so we were back at the door of the shop at precisely two minutes before nine the next morning. The gate was already pulled back, and the man with the mustache from the day before, once again wearing the down vest, was chatting amiably with another man inside. We pushed open the door and walked into a large room, quite long, with a desk in front and bookshelves in rows in the back. As we did so, the second man, turning around and noticing customers, quickly reached down and picked up a distinctive metal can with a rubber hose and nozzle coming out of the top.

"Guess I'd better be going now," he mumbled.

The man with the down vest came over. "Hello," he said.

"Hi. You can go ahead if you're busy . . ." we replied, gesturing in the general direction of the exterminator, who was already slinking discreetly toward the door.

"That's all right. He's done. We have to do it every month, or the bugs get into the books." He walked over and opened the door to a small closet.

"Can I take your coats?" Despite the use of the interrogative, this was clearly a requirement and not a courtesy. We understand the need for security in rare-book shops and ordinarily wouldn't have minded. But it was freezing in there. *He* got to wear a down vest.

"Thank you." Reluctantly, we shrugged out of our coats while the man stood there waiting. He took them and hung them up carefully. He was polite in an obligatory kind of way, as if we were a couple of boring relatives who had just shown up at his doorstep during Monday Night Football.

"Have you ever been here before?" he asked after he'd closed the closet door.

"No."

"Are you interested in anything in particular?"

"No. We'd love to look around, though."

"Well, do you know what we do here?"

"Not really."

"We specialize in Americana—eighteenth, nineteenth, and some twentieth century. We have about the best collection in the country. Do you know William Reese in New Haven?"

As it turned out, we did know William Reese. They're located in a town house near Yale. We had knocked on the door one day, and they had let us in to look around even though they told us that they run a strictly catalog and mail business and were not open to the public. When we walked in, the lunch dishes were still on the kitchen table. It's too bad they're a closed shop, because the books we did see were wonderful—in first-rate condition and at extremely fair prices. We ended up buying all three volumes of the *U.S.A.* trilogy by John Dos Passos, which Reese was selling for less than the cost of a single volume at another shop.

"Yes," we said.

"Well, basically, for Americana, it's us and William Reese."

The pride with which he said this softened him considerably. For the first time, we felt comfortable asking him his name.

"Eric Butler," he replied. "The Americana is downstairs. Upstairs is literature—American and English, eighteenth, nineteenth, and some twentieth century. I have to stay with you while you look, so why don't you start down here."

Eric turned and led us to the back of the room, where the bookcases were. He walked up the aisle on the left. "Books on books here," he said, gesturing to almost the entire far left wall of floor-to-ceiling shelves. It was, by two or three times, the most extensive books-on-books section we had ever seen.

"Look at all this A. Edward Newton!"

"Yeah, it has to gather somewhere," said Eric.

"And here's Eckel, the Dickens bibliography. I've never seen this on a shelf anywhere before."

"We have a lot of things that you won't see anywhere else. We have thirty-four thousand titles."

"How long has the store been here?"

"Thirty years here. The business has been going for sixty."

"Who's George MacManus?"

"He's dead. He was one of the original partners along with Clarence's father. Clarence took over the business when his father died."

"How long ago was that?"

"Twenty-eight years ago."

"But we thought Clarence said he was under fifty."

"He is. He was very young when he took over the shop. And don't think he wasn't resented for it," said Eric. "Everyone else in the business walked with a cane."

Eric started up the aisle. "Let me show you what else we've got. Here's Civil War, American colonial history . . ." He was at the beginning of the next aisle now. The aisles were spacious by bookshop standards. "Then the Revolutionary War, regional history, except Pennsylvania, which has its own section over here." He got to the third aisle. "The American West, over here; historical biography, twentieth-century American history, here; and, finally, crafts and decorating, art and architecture. If I can help you with anything, let me know." Eric left us to browse and went back to the desk at the front of the room.

We began in biography. As with books on books, the collection was encyclopedic. There must have been about seventy-five square feet of biographies. Big fat ones. There were books by and/or about Daniel Boone, Clara Barton, John Brown, Alexander Hamilton, Cotton Mather, James and Dolley Madison, and Gouverneur Morris. They were all hardcover and in excellent condition. We peeked into a biography of Clara Barton. "1st edition," it read. "$50." Not bad.

The collection was so exhaustive that not all the biographies were in biography. In the American Revolution section, there were four shelves of books about Benjamin Franklin, including a biography by Carl Van Doren. It didn't have a dust jacket, but was a first edition for only $25. We took it up to the desk.

"Good choice," said Eric. "That's the best book on Franklin. We always keep it in stock."

"What do you mean, that you have a stack of them upstairs or something?"

"Basically, yes," Eric relied. He almost smiled. "For certain special books like this one, we always like to have multiple copies." He paused. "By the way, were you the people who came by yesterday just when we were closing?"

"Yes. Can we go upstairs now?"

"Sure. Come on."

We went up a narrow little staircase on the side.

"How did you find out about us?" asked Eric on the way up.

"We saw your page on the Internet."

"Oh. You're the people who spoke to Clarence."

"Yes."

We had by this time reached the top of the stairs. Directly in front of us was a striking-looking room. It had high ceilings, a fine wood table in a warm hue, and beautiful old books lining the wrap-around shelves. It managed to be both comfortable and aesthetic at the same time.

There were a larger room to the left and a smaller room to the right closed off by a metal grille door.

"In there," said Eric, gesturing to the large room on the left, "is general stock. Most of the books in that room are under a hundred and twenty-five dollars. In this room," he said, pointing to the room with the table, "is better fiction, and the prices begin at about a hundred and twenty-five dollars. In that room—" the one with the metal door, "is the really good stuff. Fine literature and fine Americana."

We went into the general-stock room first. General stock at MacManus was not like general stock at most used-book stores. Most of the books were from the late nineteenth century or the early twentieth. It was interesting enough, but the pull of the other two rooms was overwhelming. Almost immediately, we were in the center room.

We had already noticed downstairs that the prices seemed extremely reasonable. Right away upstairs we noticed a first edition of *East of Eden*.

Steinbeck is a good barometer because everybody has him. *East of Eden,* for example, even in a far-less-than-perfect copy, usually goes for at least $250 and we've seen it for a good deal more than that. This was not a perfect copy, but it was in every bit as good condition as we usually see it. We opened up the front cover and saw that it was priced at $125.

"This is a very good price," we said. "Do you know that this goes for more in other places?"

"Oh, sure," Eric said with a shrug.

"Other dealers must want to buy from you."

"Feverishly," he answered. "When we go to the New York Book Fair, some of them are on us so fast we can't even get our boxes open."

"But doesn't it bother you, knowing they're going to buy it from you and then mark it up . . . that they're going to pay you one hundred dollars then turn around and sell it for two or three hundred?"

"Everyone has their own customers," Eric replied.

"But certainly you could get access to the same customers. The identity of collectors is not all that secret."

"Clarence is in the business to sell books at reasonable prices," Eric said. "That's the way he wants to work. He's not interested in wringing every last dollar out of a sale. Our customers know they'll be treated fairly. That's very important to Clarence. We pay a fair price when we buy a book, and we charge a fair price when we sell it."

We looked a little further.

"Here's *Swept Away* by Virginia Woolf," said one of us. "And, wow, it's a Hogarth Press."

Uh-oh, thought the other.

"If I were just starting out," said Eric, "I'd collect Virginia Woolf. They're available and still reasonably inexpensive, and they're charming. They were against the whole gaudy private press idea. Their books were simply done, and the designs on the jackets are understated—unusual and very interesting."

"How much is it?"

Eric looked inside. The book was in excellent condition. "This one is five hundred dollars."

"That's a very good price, don't you think so, Larry?"

"Terrific. Hey, there's *The Europeans*. Nancy, didn't you want that?"

"I always want Henry James, if we can afford it."

"Right. So how much is this one, Eric?"

"It's . . . one twenty-five. And it's one of his early novels. I've never seen a copy anywhere, except maybe at a book fair, and you can forget about those."

"We'll take it."

"Why, thank you, Larry."

"Hey, what are friends for?" *The Europeans* had just saved us $375.

"Can we look in the high-price room now?"

Eric unlocked the metal-grille door and led us through.

The contents of the high-priced room, while certainly not cheap, were nowhere near the prices that we'd seen at other shops. What made this room so extraordinary were the books themselves. Each seemed to have been chosen because of some unique feature that, taken in the aggregate, took our breath away.

We saw Aaron Burr's private journal, *Witchcraft in New England,* Benjamin Franklin's *Notes on Electricity* (a steal at $3,000), *Purchase and Exploration of Louisiana,* and, our personal favorite, a first edition of *Kidnapped,* complete with a fold-out map in the front, for $850.

When we were done, Eric took us back downstairs and went behind the desk to type out an invoice. He sat down at a computer terminal. It was part of a big, fancy system.

"Do you do a lot of Internet business?" we asked.

"Almost all of it these days," he replied. "Hardly anyone comes to the shop anymore."

When we had spoken to Richard Weatherford from Interloc, we asked him if he thought that on-line book buying was going to be a replacement or a supplement to buying books in person.

"Oh, a supplement definitely," he said. "There's no question for anyone who thinks about it. You know, they said the car was going to kill social life, then they said the telephone was going to kill conversation, then they said television was going to kill reading. The Internet might make some lower-end printed catalogs obsolete . . . catalogs are expensive to produce, and there are lots of books that don't need to be listed in catalogs . . . but going into shops and handling books? Never. Maybe some modern firsts collectors will stay at home . . . they know pretty much what they're getting . . . it's more like commodities anyway . . . but real collectors, people who love the look and the feel of the books? They're not going to stop going to shops or fairs. If anything, the Internet should increase the number of people going into shops by increasing interest in the field. The problem with the out-of-print-book business now is lots of supply and no demand."

Sorry to disagree again, but why should the Internet increase interest in a field where the product's appeal is personal and largely sensory? The Internet, it seems to us, will only increase the interest of those who are interested in used and rare books already. How many people do Mr. Weatherford or Mr. Streitfeld think will be seized with book-collecting passion as a result of seeing a listing or a description of a rare book on a computer screen, or even a high-resolution reproduction of the cover?

To attract new people, to keep the field alive, the industry needs to provide opportunities to see the books—in person—to handle the books, to speak to an educated, passionate professional, to be intoxicated by the atmosphere and the history, to get a sense of what a real library (*their* library) can be like. Otherwise, all technology will do is to access current book people, but these older collectors will die out eventually, and the circle will become smaller and smaller because no one new will be attracted.

With the Internet, you'll never be surprised, never find something you weren't already looking for, never see the fold-out map at the beginning of *Kidnapped.* The Internet is good for acquiring and amassing, but not for experiencing.

The Internet may be more functional than going to bookshops in person; it may be more efficient; it may be more private; it may be more cost-effective; and it is certainly more convenient.

It just isn't as much fun.

Chapter 9

SOTHEBY'S ANNOUNCES THE SALE OF THE
CONTENTS OF THE PARIS HOME
OF H.R.H. THE DUKE AND DUCHESS OF WINDSOR

—The Final Chapter of the most Celebrated Love Story of the 20th Century—Perhaps the Greatest Treasure House of Royal Possessions Offered At Auction—Includes "Abdication Desk" on which King Edward VIII signed the Instrument of Abdication—Over 40,000 Objects To Be Offered in 3,200 Lots—Entire Net Proceeds to go to Children's Charities—

"*Come* on, Larry. Let's do it. I'm sure there'll be books. And we've never been to Sotheby's."

"We've never been to Baghdad either. Nancy, any books here are going to cost a fortune. At the Onassis auction, you had to bid three zeros just to breathe the air."

"So what? Edward was a king. How many chances do you think we're going to have to look at a king's books? And besides, we've always had good luck at auctions before. Let's get a catalog."

"The last time we got a Sotheby's catalog, it was forty dollars, and everything was bird books. How much is it this time?"

"Ninety."

"Not a chance."

"Maybe we can get somebody else to pay for it."

"Who else are we going to get to pay for it? You mean like your father?"

"No, no. A magazine."

"Cover the auction for a magazine? Nancy, that is not a bad idea. We're hardly royal-family experts, though."

"We can read up a little. Come on. It'll be fun."

We took a couple of biographies out of the library, asked our parents and grandparents what they remembered about the duke and duchess, then called some of the dealers we knew to try and find out what their plans were for the auction.

"Nah," said Peter Stern, a high-end dealer on Newberry Street in Boston, "I don't think there's anything there for me. I'm not going to go. Why don't you call Jim Cummins?"

"They're not really my kind of books," said Kevin Rita. "Jim Cummins might be able to help you, though."

"The Windsor auction? What do you want to go to that for? They're selling *tschotckis,*" said a third dealer. "Call Jim Cummins."

"This is the kind of auction where, if you do your homework, you might actually find something," said Jim Cummins.

Jim Cummins was a man of about fifty wearing a dark, pin-striped suit and socks that flopped around his ankles. He was balding, with shoulder-length hair. On the day we were with him at his shop, James Cummins Bookseller on Madison Avenue, he was complaining about sore knees. "I play in an old fart's hockey league," he explained.

By reputation, we knew that Jim's clientele consisted mostly of wealthy collectors. He had been quoted about a month earlier in a *New York Times* article about Hollywood people who bought expensive rare books and first editions as trinkets or gifts. He was good friends with Johnny Depp and, while we were in his shop, had a bantering telephone conversation with Ricky Jaye, a magician by trade, who played the porn-film cameraman in *Boogie Nights*.

Jim Cummins' shop is the kind of place we have learned to avoid. The books are always wonderful, and we either leave miserable because we can't afford anything or miserable because we have just bought something that we couldn't afford.

"What makes you think there might be a bargain at Sotheby's?"

"The main reason," said Jim, "is that there are so many things in this auction that it is almost impossible for anyone to pay attention to everything. If there were things that slipped through at the Pamela Harriman auction and at the Jackie O auction, there will certainly be things that slip through here."

"So how do you find them?"

"Well, you've got to go to the preview and look for yourselves. But even then the stuff is going to be all over the place. Did you get a catalog?"

"Yes." We had actually secured an assignment from *Biblio,* a monthly magazine for book collectors, and the editor had sent us a copy.

"That's where to start," said Jim. "You have to go through the catalog very carefully."

Well yes, but the catalog for the Windsor collection was a three-volume, twelve-hundred page boxed set weighing over ten pounds and filled with glossy pictures of things like ashtrays, coffee tables, military buttons, Christmas cards, golf hats, shoes, and one two-page fold out color photograph of a portrait of a very small Edward on a very large horse named Forest Witch by Sir Alfred Munnings estimated at between six and eight hundred thousand dollars.

Nor were the lots segregated by type. Sotheby's had decided to organize the auction room by room, as the items had appeared in the Windsors' Paris villa. Since books—and there were thousands of them—were scattered all over the house, they were scattered all over the catalog as well, most with scant descriptions, such as:

> 1773 **Popular Fiction and Literature**
> A collection of approximately 43 reading volumes, including works by Agatha Christie, Michael Crichton, Rex Stout, Dashiell Hammett, George V. Higgins, Gore Vidal, and others, mostly 20th-century, some paper bound. A few of the volumes have ownership inscriptions or presentation inscriptions (e.g., Jacqueline Susann, *The Love Machine,* 1969, inscribed "To the Duke and Duchess of Windsor, All my very best Jacqueline Susann.") $300–500

Some lots contained in excess of one hundred books with no indication of condition at all. So, while the estimated values seemed reasonable—almost too reasonable—without seeing the books themselves, there was no way of knowing if you were dealing with a pristine copy or something that the Windsors' beloved pugs had used for a dog toy.

Jim had his own catalog fetched for him by an assistant. His copy was dog-eared in at least fifty places, with little yellow stickies placed in as many more.

"Obviously you think there's some good stuff here."

"Definitely," he said with a nod for emphasis. "There are great association copies. There's a presentation copy to Wallis from Andy Warhol where he spelled 'Duchess' wrong. There are all sorts of things. And then, of course, there are the Churchills."

The Churchills to which Jim was referring was lot 1386, "A Remarkable Presentation Set" of first editions of *The World Crisis,* a history of the First World War. There were six volumes, each inscribed by Churchill to the then prince of Wales, with three extremely affectionate letters laid in. The set was valued at thirty to forty thousand dollars, which was more than twice as much as any other book lot in the entire collection.

"A first-edition Churchill association copy signed to the duke will be worth something because it is Churchill, and it is better to have a book signed by Churchill to the duke than by Churchill to Joe Schmoe," said Jim. "Steve Forbes collects Churchill. But the value will be because of Churchill, not the duke."

"So you think the Churchills will get the forty thousand."

"Oh, they'll go for two or three times that," said Jim with a wave of his hand. "And if someone like Bill Gates decides this set is something he just has to have . . ."

"So, if there's so much good stuff, how come there's so little interest in the trade?"

"What are you talking about?"

"We talked to a number of other dealers, and they said they weren't bidding on anything."

"Like who?" asked Jim, perking up.

"Oh, Peter Stern, for instance."

"Peter's bidding," said Jim. "He's bidding through me."

The telephone rang. Jim was told that it was an overseas call. He excused himself, picked up the phone, and began a conversation with someone named Dieter. To give him some privacy, we got up and began to browse.

This was a mistake.

Jim's books, as we feared, were excellent. There were sets of Henry James, Mark Twain, and Dickens, lots of beautifully bound eighteenth- and nineteenth-century literature, sporting books, art books, and on the walls, sketches by Dante Gabriel Rossetti, including one of Janey Morris. Even worse, nothing was overpriced. If anything, Jim's prices were a bit less than those we had experienced at comparable dealers.

Jim hung up the telephone. We were standing by the shelves, holding a beautiful red-leather volume with raised bands and gilt edges. It was a book we had been looking for, but had never seen in anywhere near this condition. It was two hundred dollars.

"For some reason, people don't collect *Trilby* much anymore," said Jim, with a nod toward the book in our hands. "That's why it's not that expensive. It's funny, because when *Trilby* came out, it was a huge best-seller. That copy was bound by Sangorski and Sutcliffe."

In our earlier days as book buyers this would have been the moment at which there would be a lot of hemming and hawing and some meaningless platitudes, after which we would buy the book. We're much more sophisticated now. We just shut up and gave Jim our credit card.

"So . . . do you think this auction is going to be like the Onassis auction?"

"Sotheby's certainly hopes so," Jim replied, running our card through his machine. "But I'm not so sure. At the Jackie O auction, even books that weren't interesting went for hundreds or thousands of dollars more than their value . . . Do you want me to mail this to you so you'll save the tax?"

"Uh, sure."

"Anyway, that's not going to happen here. The duke's books might not go for more than market value."

"Why not?"

"Well, there are a lot of people who don't like the Windsors. They're not exactly beloved figures."

"But isn't this supposed to be the most celebrated love story of the twentieth century?"

"Not to everyone."

It didn't take a lot of figuring to realize that Sotheby's had a lot riding on the Windsors. Ads for the auction had appeared in major newspapers, in art magazines, and in publications that catered to antique lovers or collectors. Articles about the duke and duchess had popped up with regularity, and most of them were heavily laden with references to romance or style.

Publicity like that doesn't come cheap, and what's more, the auction was going to tie up Sotheby's entire New York premises for almost a month. They had even hired a set designer who specialized in museum exhibits to create a theme for the preview and help arrange the display. The job of cataloging, shipping, and then laying out forty thousand items must have been Herculean, and while many of these items were sure to be sold for thousands of dollars, others—photographs, address labels, and the like—were more problematic.

With this investment to protect and with the enormous success of the Onassis auction as precedent, Sotheby's reached out to segments of the public not generally associated with the venerable auction house. One night, for example, we were flipping through the television channels when suddenly we stopped. It was QVC, the home shopping network.

On the television screen were two people sitting in armchairs with a little table between them. On the right was a man in his thirties. He was very tall, had brown hair, and was wearing a fashionable light brown suit. He spoke in an easy, practiced manner and had a nonaccented, media-trained voice. On the left was a perky, attractive, dark-haired woman of about thirty, dressed in high boots and an expensive South Moulton Street ensemble, complete with slit skirt. Her accent was pure U.K. and impeccable. Underneath was a transparency identifying her as Kerry Taylor, head of Sotheby's Textiles and Wardrobe Division.

On the table were copies of the three massive, midnight blue paperback volumes that constituted the Windsor catalog. The man on the right, whom Kerry called David in a manner that implied that they had been friends for years, held up one of them in his hand. On the cover was a photograph of the duke and the duchess in soft focus. The duke was standing, looking aristocratic, and the duchess was sitting in front of him, her hands folded in her lap. The title read, "The Duke & Duchess of Windsor, THE PUBLIC COLLECTIONS.

"They had great style, didn't they, Kerry?" enthused David.

"Oh, yeeeesss," Kerry agreed, smiling fetchingly and giving a little toss of her head. "Everywhere they went, they set the fashion standard."

The camera moved to a full-page picture of an unspeakably hideous green-plaid suit, the kind of thing characters in 1970s black exploitation films used to wear getting in and out of Cadillacs with fur interiors and a half-ton of chrome along the sides.

"Oh, I'm so glad you've shown that one, David," Kerry continued. "It's one of my very favorites." Kerry, one got the feeling, could keep her smile and good cheer on the back rail of the *Titanic*.

"This is one of the great romances in history, isn't it?" continued David eagerly.

"Oh, yeeessss," Kerry replied. "One of the *great* romances."

"This is the man who abdicated the throne, gave up an empire for the woman he loved," David prompted.

"Yes, he did," agreed Kerry.

"And not everything at this auction is going to go for millions of dollars!" said David. "Most people think that an auction like this is out of reach to them. But there are lots of things that the *average* person could afford, aren't there? Wouldn't you say, Kerry, that the *average* person should be interested in this auction?"

"Oh, definitely, David. There is certainly something here for *everyone.*"

David turned to the camera. "This will be a wonderful auction, and if you want the catalog, which is a collector's item in itself—even if you can't attend the auction, you'll want the catalog, it's filled with wonderful color photographs of one of the great romantic couples in history—isn't that so—"

"Oh, yesss—"

"—If you want a copy of this catalog for yourself, at the special shopping-channel price, just call the number that appears on your screen."

Another transparency appeared over Kerry's right shoulder. It gave a telephone number to call for the Windsor catalog, and the special shopping-channel price of $110. But you could pay in two easy installments of $55 each, and, as David emphasized continually, "S&H [shipping and handling to the uninitiated] is *free!* And that's not very much at all," he added, "to own a piece of the most celebrated love affair of the twentieth century!"

The legend of the most celebrated love affair of the twentieth century began on the evening of December 11, 1936, when then-king Edward VIII announced in a radio broadcast to his subjects that he was giving up the throne to which he had ascended only ten months earlier, for "the woman I love."

The woman Edward loved was an American named Wallis Warfield Simpson. For the next thirty-five years Edward, now the duke of Windsor, and Mrs. Simpson, the duchess, lived side by side and were centerpieces of jet-set society on both sides of the Atlantic. They were photographed by Cecil Beaton and Man Ray; their movements were reported on in *Vogue* and *Vanity Fair*; their dinners were the quintessence of elegance and good taste; and their houseguests included Somerset Maugham, Noel Coward, King Leopold of Belgium, and Harold Nicholson.

This was an unlikely outcome to both of their lives.

Edward, of course, was raised to be a king, and Bessie Wallis Warfield was a poor relation of a wealthy, old-line Maryland family. Her father died when she was five, and her mother made ends meet by renting out rooms and living on the charity of rich cousins.

Before Wallis Warfield became Mrs. Simpson, she had first been Mrs. Earl Winfield Spencer. When marriage to Win, a handsome American naval officer with a promising career dissipated by drink, did not work out, Wallis left him. Her next serious flirtation was with an Argentine diplomat whom she did not marry. When this affair had run its course, Wallis scouted around awhile before setting her sights on Ernest Simpson, the respectable upper-middle-class heir to his family's shipping business. They were married in 1928 and settled in London.

Mrs. Simpson met Edward, prince of Wales, three years later. Although it seems that Edward was not immediately taken with Mrs. Simpson, by early 1932, she and the prince were taking long weekends together.

From the first, Mrs. Simpson was generally viewed by those in British high society as a sexual predator, a kind of Becky Sharp of the 1930s. There were even widely circulated rumors that when she had spent time in the Orient, she engaged Chinese concubines to teach her some advanced sexual techniques. Edward's sexual initiation, on the other hand, did not occur until his midtwenties, and even then his advisors had to procure the services of a prostitute to ease him into manhood. After a couple of brief flings, he had engaged in an affair with an older married woman, Mrs. Freda Dudley Ward, which had lasted for ten years. Once Mrs. Simpson entered the picture, however, Mrs. Dudley Ward was cut off so abruptly and summarily that she could not even get through to the prince on the telephone.

Edward's affair with Mrs. Simpson continued quite publicly, at least among the upper classes, during the last four years of his tenure as prince of Wales. During this period, Mr. Simpson was the very model of British patriotism and probity. If it bothered him that his wife was *schtupping* the prince, he never showed it. In fact, so understanding was Ernest that one wag declared, "He has laid down his wife for his country."

Then, in 1936, Edward's father, King George V, died, and Edward assumed the throne. Whoever now married Edward would become the queen of England.

Divorce proceedings began immediately. Since it obviously wouldn't do for a future queen to be named as the accused in such an action, Mrs. Simpson instead arranged to sue Mr. Simpson on grounds of adultery. Ernest, always willing to help out, obligingly allowed himself to be caught in the act with someone else.

To try and preserve some aura of propriety, it was decided that Mrs. Simpson was to be out of the country while awaiting her decree. It was only after she had been safely packed off to the Continent that the bomb was dropped on Edward. No one was going to allow him to marry Wallis and remain king—not the queen mother, not the prime minister, and not the clergy.

By the time Mrs. Simpson was officially divorced, Edward was distraught with loneliness. He spent hours on the telephone pining after her and listening as she complained about the shabby treatment to which she was being subjected.

So Edward abdicated. Then, after the radio broadcast, he quietly stole away from Great Britain in the dead of night. Thinking that he would still remain a vibrant and valued member of the royal family, he made virtually no provision for his future role.

As the duke of Windsor, Edward never lived in England again. During World War II, he was sent to the Bahamas so that his notorious sympathies for Hitler and Nazism could not be exploited by the Germans. (During the Battle of Britain, he is known for having pestered Churchill to get his former domestic staff, most of whom by this time were in active service, released from the military and sent to the Bahamas on the grounds that it would be "a serious handicap starting with a new valet.")

After the war, Edward returned to England occasionally for short visits or to attend funerals, but Wallis did not accompany him, nor was she ever received by a member of the royal family. They lived in various places—New York, the south of France—until finally, they settled in Paris, at No. 4 Rue du Champs d'Entrainement, a Louis XVI–style villa, near the Bois de Boulogne.

The duke died in 1972 and the duchess in 1986. In her will, she specified that all proceeds of her estate were to be left to charity, specifically the Institut Pasteur. The duchess's jewelry and a good deal of the most valuable furniture and art were sold at auction soon after her death (for over $50 million) and the proceeds duly applied.

The remainder of the duke's and duchess's possessions were purchased by a single buyer who also secured a long-term lease on the house. This buyer, Mohamed al-Fayed, an Egyptian expatriate, was the owner of Harrods. He also owned country estates, employed members of the British ruling class, including Lady Spencer, Princess Diana's mother, and made enormous philanthropic and cultural contributions to British society. His brother, Ali, owned Turnbull and Asser, shirtmakers to the aristocracy.

Al-Fayed promised that he would maintain, in perpetuity, the downstairs floors of the Paris residence exactly as they had been during the duke's and duchess's lifetimes. The house would become a private museum in honor of the Windsors. If he used the house at all, he would live in the attic.

Mohamed al-Fayed applied for British citizenship in the early 1990s. It seemed, however, that while those who rule in the U.K. liked Mohamed al-Fayed's money and they liked his store and they liked his brother's shirts, they did not like him. His request for citizenship was turned down.

Some months later, Mohamed al-Fayed's son, Emad, "Dodi," began what was destined to be a tragic romance with Diana, princess of Wales. Shortly after they started seeing each other seriously, Mohamed al-Fayed contacted Sotheby's and put all of the Windsor possessions right down to the orange-and-red-checked socks and the solid-silver dog dishes on the block. When asked why he was taking such a precipitous course, al-Fayed answered simply, "My family is expanding, and I need the space."

In a sign that, six decades later, the British public had still not forgiven Edward, one of the first decisions Sotheby's made was to hold the auction in their New York premises, rather than in their home base in London.

Sotheby's New York occupied a three-story granite-and-glass building on the far east side of Manhattan, stretching between

Seventy-first and Seventy-second Streets and running halfway from York Avenue to Sutton Place. There was a plate-glass entranceway in the front, through which you could see a white-marble staircase with SOTHEBY'S emblazoned on the side, and over which was hanging the flag of Great Britain alongside the Stars and Stripes. Just to the left of the stairs was a window, nearly twenty feet wide and two stories high, filled entirely by a blue banner proclaiming, THE COLLECTION OF THE DUKE & DUCHESS OF WINDSOR in foot-high letters across the top, with a portrait of the Windsors in profile, staring off toward East Harlem.

A press preview was held the day before the exhibition was to be opened to the public. We got there about ten minutes early and waited in line just inside the front door. Martha MacCallum, a correspondent from CNBC, wearing a dark blue pin-striped suit, was behind us, and the technicians for Channel 2 News, wearing filthy jeans and sneakers, were in front.

After leaving our coats in the checkroom, we were handed a press kit, and instructed to walk up the stairs, past snow white tulips and peonies in huge stone pots flanking a placard inscribed with the Windsors' coat of arms. On the second floor was a holding area near the General Inquiries and Catalogue desk. To the right, white-jacketed waiters stood behind long tables heaped with enormous trays of mini-sticky buns and *ruglach,* delicately sliced coffee cakes, and bite-size muffins. There were large glass pitchers filled with fresh-squeezed orange and grapefruit juice and gleaming silver urns of steaming coffee. We seemed to be the only people there without little plastic badges around their necks proclaiming their affiliation with a network or major print organization.

After about ten minutes of milling and munching, we were ushered by a number of fashionably dressed, smiling women in black suits and heels to a large, circular open area to the left. There in the center, under discreet lighting, in front of an eight-foot-square scrim with an excerpt of Edward's abdication speech printed in red script, was a platform on which stood the abdication desk. On top of the desk were two photos of the duchess on a little stand, a beat-up old red-leather letter box with the words THE KING stamped on them in gilt, some orange tulips in a little silver vase, and a sword. Projected on the walls behind the scrim were the royal seal and the following epigrams, repeated over and over again in sequence like those movie quizzes that they run before the previews in your local multiplex:

My friend
With thee to live alone
Methinks were better than to own
A crown, a sceptre and a throne

—*Alfred, Lord Tennyson*

Coming events
cast their shadows before them

—*Wallis Simpson*

My dear fine baby
was brought in . . .
The child was very good

—*Queen Victoria*

Eventually, a thin, attractive woman with frizzy blonde hair, wearing a dark blue suit cut two inches above the knee and a string of golf-ball-size pearls, walked to the platform and stood in front of the desk. We recognized her from the news stories about the Onassis auction as Diana Brooks, president and chief executive officer of Sotheby's. Technicians with mini-cams on their shoulders began jockeying for position in order to get a clear shot. In deference to the event, they whispered, "Excuse me" before shoving us out of the way with roller-derby-caliber elbows.

Diana Brooks smiled.

"Welcome, everyone. For Sotheby's this has been a long-awaited moment. We have been working on this collection for five years, and then it had to be put off because of the tragic deaths of Dodi Fayed and Princess Diana . . ." She paused a moment before continuing. "Unlike the Onassis auction, this will be entirely open to the public, and there will be tours every day of the ten-day viewing session. Mohamed al-Fayed has renamed the foundation the Dodi Fayed Foundation, and the net proceeds of the auction will go to children's causes, which were very important to Dodi Fayed and Princess Diana. There are over forty thousand objects . . . this was the greatest love story of the twentieth century . . ."

After some more introductory comments from people who had actually worked with the collection, we were allowed to wander about. We saw desks and chairs and beds and table linens and paintings and vases. There were display cases filled with parasols and fans, including ostrich feathers; piles of silken lingerie bags and a set of twenty-six pairs of eyeglasses and cases, some of them jeweled. There were hats with feathers and hats with bows and a black hat with a veil that the duchess had obviously worn to the duke's funeral. There were at least three hundred pairs of gloves ranging from black velvet to apricot satin. In a back room downstairs was a wall of shoes in a shelved glass case, some of them so worn that you could see the duchess's bunion marks right there at eye level. Along another wall were over one hundred framed photos of the duke in various postures and costumes. A little farther down, all of their clothes (including the green plaid suit) had been placed on headless mannequins grouped together, as if at a macabre cocktail party.

Like everything else at this auction, the books, by virtue of sheer number, were overwhelming. Although some of the more unusual or expensive volumes were in their own display cases, literally thousands of books were locked up in mirrored, glass-enclosed shelves with only the spines visible. Some of the books were doubled, one row placed directly behind another, so there was no way of even knowing what the ones in the back row were. Over 90 percent of the lots contained multiple books. These were bundled together with strips of thin black ribbon. Some lots contained so many books, it took five or six bundles to display them. The only way to know which bundles belonged to which lot was by a tag that protruded from the top of one of the books, which noted the lot number and, underneath, the total number of books in the lot. For example, there were four tags that read "1773," each with a "43" underneath.

We immediately made our way to the glass case containing the Churchills. This set had been given two full pages in the catalog, each of which featured a color photograph in which the books appeared bright, crisp, and shiny. The only description noted that the set was "a bit rubbed."

Seeing the books in person was a shock. "A bit rubbed" was extremely generous. The bindings were dull, not bright and there were chips at the top of the spines and even a couple of tears in the leather.

"Do you think even someone like Steve Forbes is going to pay eighty thousand dollars for these?"

"Sure. You heard what Jim said. That kind of collector doesn't care about condition, only association."

In the same display case were some other Churchill memorabilia, including a set of *The Second World War* without dust jackets, which was inscribed by Churchill to the then Duke in 1947 with substantially less affection than in *The World Crisis* ("I hope Your Royal Highness will accept this first volume of my war story," it says in *The Gathering Storm*) and which were valued at $8,000–$10,000. But even this was warm in contrast to a book that was open to its title page and whose inscription read succinctly: "To The Duchess of Windsor from Winston S. Churchill 1949."

The only non-Churchill item in the case was a presentation copy of John F. Kennedy's *Profiles in Courage*. In the catalog, this was featured in a half-page color photograph with the book open to the front endpaper, where the dedication appears. It was valued at $2,000–$3,000 and described as "publisher's cloth; tail edge worn. Dust jacket; some wear."

"Some wear" was, once again, a gross understatement. *Profiles in Courage* looked like something you'd buy for a couple of dollars at a used-book store. It would not have been described as better than "very good" in even the most optimistic dealer catalog.

We walked away disheartened. Even putting aside the historic importance of the books, they had been gifts to the Windsors, tokens of esteem from acclaimed individuals. Before the abdication, Churchill had been one of Edward's closest friends. We couldn't help but feel that it said something about the duke and duchess that they had apparently thrown these books around like someone chucking a John Grisham paperback onto the bottom shelf of the nightstand.

The lots containing reading copies were even worse. Most of the hardcovers lacked dust jackets, and a large number of the paperbacks were in outrightly poor condition. The titles were not especially arresting, either. This was also disappointing, since when we had looked through the catalog the lots containing the reading copies were the only ones where we thought we might be able to get something interesting at a price we could afford. But even at the low end of the estimated price, we weren't going to pay $300 for beat-up, unjacketed copies of *Tai-Pan* or *Inside Russia Today*.

Of all the people who had been exposed to the onslaught of publicity or purchased one of the thirty-one thousand copies of the catalog that Sotheby's had sold, only a tiny percentage, we knew, would be able to attend the preview. We wondered how those who bid solely on the basis of the catalog would feel when the books themselves came into their possession.

We continued to browse through the cases, although there had seemed to be nothing else in the catalog that merited our attention. One case, however, did contain a large number of attractive books in leather bindings. They were in decent condition—far better condition than the reading copies, or even the Churchills. There were a set of Jane Austen, a number of Conrads, Thackerays, and a set by someone called Captain Marryat. When we looked at the tags, we realized that all of these books came from a single lot.

> 1767 **English Literature**
> An attractive collection of approximately 18 works in 128 volumes, mostly sets of works of standard English authors, including Jane Austen, Thomas Carlyle, Joseph Conrad, Walter Scott, and Captain Marryat, mostly 18th- and 19th-century, mostly half or full morocco or calf.
> $1,500–2,000

How could 128 leather-bound books in good condition by well-known authors be valued at $1,500–$2,000? That was $15 a book. A passable leather-bound set of Jane Austen alone usually runs $750–$1,000, and she only wrote six novels.

"If there was no provenance, we valued the books at what we thought they would sell for in the market," said Selby Kiffer.

We had gone back to the General Inquiries Desk and asked to speak to someone in the book department. We got Selby on the phone, and he agreed to come down from his office on the third floor to talk to us. He was a polite, soft-spoken, bearded man of about forty, dressed in a light gray suit. He was of medium height and build and had a gentle quality about him.

We led him over to the case where we had seen lot number 1767. He walked soundlessly, as befits a man with a graduate degree in library science.

"None of these have ownership inscriptions," said Selby, although he did note that Sotheby's had glued a bookplate on the front cover of each volume identifying it as part of the collection of the duke and duchess of Windsor.

"Still," we said, "these books seem undervalued when compared to the reading copies," and we mentioned the lot with the Jacqueline Susann.

"It's the inscription," Selby replied. "We thought that it was a little unusual to have a copy of *The Love Machine* inscribed to the Windsors."

"So you don't think 1767 is valued low?"

"Well, we're certainly not trying to discourage people from bidding."

Selby took us around, showing us the items for which he had a personal affinity. "The militaria are wonderful," he said, "and there are bits of royal-family history that almost never come on the market." He spoke with the kind of quiet enthusiasm you only find in people who love what they do.

"Do you collect yourself?"

Selby smiled. "I don't anymore. It's hard to collect when you work here. It kind of emphasizes how low on the collecting scale you can afford to be. These days, I collect campaign buttons."

He led us to one of the glass cases that we had skimmed past and pointed to a pea green book with no dust jacket on the top shelf.

The title was *Pig-Sticking and Hog-Hunting: A Complete Account for Sportsmen,* and the author was Sir Michael Baden-Powell. "I think it's interesting to have a book with a title like that inscribed to the duke by the founder of the Boy Scouts," said Selby.

Then we asked how to go about bidding if we decided to take a shot at 1767.

"You can bid by paddle or by order."

"We don't like to bid by order. If we're the only bidders, we can end up paying a lot more than we have to."

"Oh, no," he said. "We don't do that here. If you put in an order bid for, say, three thousand dollars, we'd open at the low estimate, and if there were no other bids, that's what you'd get it for."

"So, in other words, if we put in an order bid, it would only be the most we're willing to pay."

"That's right," Selby nodded. "We think that's the fairest way."

"Or we can bid by paddle in the room."

"If you like."

One hundred and twenty-eight books for two thousand dollars. Hmmmm.

The opening session was scheduled to begin at six-thirty, but we decided to arrive at five o'clock. Who knew? Maybe they were going to let people in early and serve those little appetizers again. If not, we'd have time for a cup of coffee or a glass of wine before we went inside.

The evening started with a good omen. Less than two blocks from Sotheby's, just as we were about to pull into a parking garage, incredibly, we found a legal parking spot right on the street, in front of an apartment building with a doorman no less. So, already twenty dollars to the good, we got out and happily sauntered down the street, dressed appropriately, or so we thought, in a dark suit and a long, lace cocktail dress.

When we got to York Avenue, we saw through the glass entranceway that people were already packed on to the marble staircase and the line stretched out onto the sidewalk. In the street, directly in front of the entrance, were two platforms, one with a little tent over which was emblazoned CNN NEWSOURCE with the logo of a satellite dish, and the other bare except for three director's chairs, a camera, and some lights.

The people in line were decently but not extravagantly dressed. We were a little surprised. Maybe it was the Sotheby's aura, but we had expected a hefty dose of black-tie and the kind of evening gowns that they show on the runways in Milan.

When we told the doorman we were press, he directed us around the corner to a small side entrance on Seventy-second Street. The line here consisted of the same unsmiling on-air correspondents and sullen technicians whom we had encountered at the press preview. A number of harried-looking young men and women with little Sotheby's badges were running up and down the block talking mostly to each other, and one stupendously bored New York City police officer was leaning against the building with his legs crossed and his hands in his pockets, making it a point not to smile at anyone.

A man got into line behind us. He was in his fifties, with a gray beard, a rumpled gray suit, a maroon-and-white wide-striped shirt, and a maroon tie.

"Hi, I'm Arthur," he said affably. "I'm here for the books. What are you here for?"

This was the first time during our venture into the world of the working press that anyone had made any overture to us at all.

"Uh, we're here for the books, too," we replied.

"Great," said Arthur. Arthur, as it turned out, was not with the press at all. He was tagging along with his wife, who did some freelance radio for the BBC. He had made arrangements in advance, but was now upset because someone had just told him he couldn't have a paddle in the press area. His wife, Susan, was off straightening it out.

"I collect English history," he said. "I sort of specialize in the Reformation, but I'm interested in anything of historic value.

"There's some really good stuff here," he continued, taking a list out of his pocket that had been torn from a legal pad. " 'The Prince of Wales copy of the Order of Service for the Coronation of His Parents,' that's a good one," he said. "It's beautifully bound. But what I'd really like is that big proclamation, the one by King George VI where he created the title of duke of Windsor . . . there'd never been anything like that before, they weren't really sure how to do it. That one comes with a terrific pendant wax seal of King George attached to the proclamation by a green-silk ribbon. I collect seals when I can. I have one from Henry III."

Arthur laughed and shook his head. "I'll never get anything, though. The valuations are ridiculously low. Everything's going to go for much more than they're showing in the book."

By this, we took it to mean that Arthur was there much as we were—entertaining a fantasy about coming away with something but lacking the means to make it happen.

Just before we were to be let in, Arthur's wife, Susan, showed up with a paddle for Arthur. She was a small, friendly woman wearing a plain tan blouse and a brown skirt. As Arthur introduced us, Susan looked us up and down.

"Oh. You dressed," she said.

Arthur clutched his paddle contentedly as we moved toward the door. Just inside, our names were checked against a list, and we were given press badges and ushered up a set of back stairs.

The auction was being held in the main hall, which, during the preview, had been partitioned to hold the scrim, the platform with the abdication desk, and several rooms of the exhibition. For opening night they had rolled the partitions away and set up rows and rows of folding chairs, each about twenty-five across, more than twelve hundred chairs in all. There was an aisle in the middle and along the sides, and, although all the tickets were free, the first fifteen rows were marked RESERVED.

In the front of the room was a long, two-tiered podium, covered with a dark blue cloth, the same color as on the catalogs. Attached to the cloth were signs that read, "Los Angeles" and "Chicago," manned by fourteen Sotheby's employees with telephones at their ears. The Munnings portrait hung behind them. Flags and banners from the collection hung from the ceiling and on the facades overhead. A lectern for the auctioneer was set just off center to the right, and at the far right was another table with at least ten more employees on the telephone. Between the lectern and the podium was a revolving platform, divided into four sections, a kind of giant Lazy Susan, which was used to display whichever lot was to be up for bid.

High on the wall was a screen on which was projected the image of whichever lot was at the front of the Lazy Susan. Immediately to the right of that was a tote board with a big SOTHEBY'S across the top, where the current lot and current bid in dollars would be displayed. Underneath were Br. Pounds, Swiss Francs, French Francs, Ger. Marks, Lira, and Yen, all immediately updating as the bids changed.

The press area was squeezed off against the far left wall, under a balcony and behind a row of pillars, separated from the bidders by velvet ropes, which, we had been told, we were forbidden to cross without escort by a Sotheby's press officer. Two low platforms had been set up in the back to allow clear shots for the at least twenty-five video cameras that had been set up. There must have been 150 press people squeezed in like cattle. We were lucky enough to grab a couple of folding chairs that had been tossed across by the staff like crusts of bread to POWs, but once we sat down, we realized that, because of the cameras rolling behind us, we couldn't get up again. Next to us sat a henna-haired woman named Valérie from *Le Monde*, and next to her, Arthur and Susan had grabbed two chairs.

We watched as the audience moved in and took seats. Even with hundreds of people filing in, the room remained quiet enough to have a conversation without raising your voice. The people in the rows behind the reserved section kept turning around, trying to see if anyone wonderful was coming in, but no one did.

The press people also seemed to have failed to have been caught up in the event. "So," we heard one woman passing behind us say in a bored voice to another, "were you at Camp David?"

There was money, though. Directly across from us was a couple in their late thirties who were perusing a catalog. The man was dressed in gray slacks and a tweed sport jacket, and the woman was in a muddy teal pants suit, both outfits looking as though they had been bought off the rack at Syms. The woman, however, was wearing a wedding ring with a sapphire surrounded by diamonds. The sapphire was so large that it was surprising that she could lift her hand without assistance. Directly behind her sat a woman in her sixties, with stylishly cut blonde hair and the figure of a woman in her thirties. She wore a wedding ring with a diamond surrounded by diamonds. The sapphire could have fit inside the diamond.

At precisely 6:29, with the entire back section of the hall still empty and even about 20 percent of the reserved area unoccupied, Diana Brooks suddenly appeared at the rear of the hall. Instead of the usual Sotheby's black, tonight she wore a satiny, bright red suit. She strode down the side aisle and over to the lectern like a fireball.

The difference in her demeanor was striking. Where, in her remarks at the press briefing, she had been diffident, even halting, tonight she was all eloquence. She arrived at the podium, lifted the hammer, and RAP!

"Good evening, ladies and gentlemen. We begin tonight an historic auction. All of us at Sotheby's are honored to be here. The rules of the auction are as follows:

"For this evening's session, we will take bids in our main hall in New York, and simultaneously in our offices in Chicago and Los Angeles . . ." ("But not in London," whispered one of the reporters.) "All lots are sold 'as is.' By 'as is' we mean . . ." She spent about two minutes explaining the rules in a practiced rat-a-tat, and read a note from Mohamed al-Fayed explaining why he was not attending in person but how pleased he was that all this money would go to his son's and Princess Diana's favorite charities. And then she got right to it.

The giant Lazy Susan turned to reveal a cameo-size photograph of a baby in a white nightgown.

"We will begin with lot number one, a portrait of Prince Edward in his christening robes. We begin the bidding at one thousand five hundred dollars. One thousand five hundred, seven fifty, two thousand, on the phone at twenty-two fifty . . ."

She continued taking bids, nodding, pointing, cajoling. She could be simultaneously firm, sweet, even flirtatious. She knew when to go fast and when to allow the bidders time until they could not stop themselves from bidding that extra $2,500. In the end, lot number 1 sold for $24,000, eight times the high end of the valuation. With the 15-percent buyer's premium, the final cost was $27,600.

Lot number 2, a silver child's mug, went for $11,000 against a high estimate of $3,000; number 3, a photograph of the baby Edward with his grandmother, Queen Victoria, $7,000 against $1,200; and on and on. Lots were regularly selling for five, sometimes more than ten times their high estimates.

Then she arrived at "Lot number fifteen, The Prince of Wales copy of the Order of Service for the Coronation of His Parents. The bidding will begin at thirty-five hundred . . ." The bid was $7,250, when suddenly Diana Brooks said, "Seventy-five hundred. New bidder, on the right."

We looked in the direction of her eyes and saw that the new bidder was . . . Arthur.

"Seven seventy-five, on the phone. Eight thousand." It was Arthur again. She lifted the hammer. "Fair warning. At eight thousand dollars." Diana Brooks always seemed to say, "Fair warning" when she was disappointed with the bid. In this case, the high estimate was $7,000. Then RAP! "Sold! For eight thousand dollars."

There were a number of rollicking sales. A Cecil Beaton portrait of the duchess looking languorous and wearing a yellow-and-blue flowered dress, valued at $10,000–$15,000, went for $120,000. No "fair warning" this time. "Cecil would be proud," Diana Brooks beamed. But the highlight of the evening was undoubtedly lot number 58, a 2¾"-square box, wrapped in white paper with a white ribbon, inside of which was a piece of the duke's and duchess's wedding cake. This item had been valued at $500–$1,000, but after furious bidding was sold to Benjamin and Amanda Yim, a young couple from San Francisco, for $26,000. When asked what he intended to do with the cake, Mr. Yim replied, "Well, I'm sure not going to eat it." The underbidder was the Ripley's Believe-It-or-Not Museum.

Then there was lot number 54, the proclamation with the seal. Arthur got that one too, for $19,000, against a high valuation of $15,000—not bad, especially when you consider the price of a piece of inedible wedding cake. All in all, with buyer's premium and sales tax, the man in the rumpled gray suit had dropped a quick $33,500 in about forty minutes.

"Books are always the best deal," Arthur said afterward. "Look at the books next to the Cecil Beaton portrait. And all because you can't hang them on the wall."

Session two, "The Royal Family: Photographs; Books; Medals and Coins," was Friday morning at ten, and if not for the Windsor blue hanging all over the place, someone could easily not have known that this was the same auction. The entire rear section of seats had been removed and a partition rolled in to create a smaller hall. In this smaller hall, no more than two hundred people sat quietly as items were put up for bids. Most of the participants had notated catalogs open in their laps and were following the bidding closely. Jim Cummins was there, sitting at the rear of the hall, marking his place in his dog-eared catalog with his paddle.

As soon as they got to the books, Arthur's theory seemed once again to be borne out. None of the books went for the stratospheric multiples that were regularly bid for knick-knacks, and one or two books did not even reach the low estimate. Jim, in fact, got lot number 177, a handsome leather-bound book called *Shires and Provinces*, valued at $1,200–$1,600, for $750. (As it turned out, this was below the reserve price and was thus withdrawn, although Jim got it anyway by making a side deal with Sotheby's after the session was concluded. We learned later that he bought a number of other items in the same way.)

Lots that contained multiple books fetched a good deal more than individual volumes, but even in these cases nothing provoked even a fraction of the insanity as had the wedding cake. Ordinarily, we might have been depressed that books did so poorly, but our depression was tempered somewhat since, as outlandish as it seemed, it meant that maybe, just maybe, lot number 1767 might be within our reach.

Friday turned out to be an anomaly, however. On Saturday, there were at least five hundred people in the audience, and the crowd was even more suburban than on the first night, filled with eager-looking women in Armani sitting next to glum, resigned-looking men.

Before the bidding got underway, we overheard a conversation between two press representatives.

"So, did they get anybody?" asked the first.

"Nah," replied the second, whose badge identified her as being from a national magazine, "just Tommy Hilfiger the first night. He spent a lot of money and bought some really ugly stuff."

At this session, Tommy had lots of company. This was *tschotcki* day, when ugly little paintings went for $3,000 against a high estimate of $200, and a 5¾" electroplated ashtray, to a big round of applause, sold for $11,000 against a high estimate of $400.

There had been applause after the bidding for the wedding cake, too. And for the Beaton painting. In fact, every time someone paid a ridiculous amount of money for something that Sotheby's experts had determined was worth orders of magnitude less, the audience applauded. It was a little confusing. We never could figure out if the applause was for whoever spent all that money or for Sotheby's for getting them to do it.

We took Sunday off, but Monday morning's session was one that we would not miss. It was then that the Munnings portrait, the inscribed set of Churchills, *Profiles in Courage,* and lots of other books were to be put up. We expected a repeat of Saturday, but to our relief, it seemed to be a crowd much more like Friday's—sparse, sophisticated, intelligent. We could pick out a number of book dealers, including Jim Cummins, who was there in a blue blazer and tie.

As the bidding got closer to lot number 1339, the Munnings portrait, a real sense of anticipation filled the room. Then, amid complete quiet, it began, at a half million dollars. Within seconds it was over a million and a few seconds after that, at a million three. We watched with some fascination as the bidding topped a million five. We didn't know beans about art, but, to us, the Munnings portrait simply *wasn't any good.* The horse and the figure of Edward were detailed enough, but the features of both were utterly lacking in animation. And the large tree to the right, just past the horse's behind, had been done in large, undefined blobs of greens and browns, like something that might have come out of an old ladies' art school.

Our critical analysis did not stop the bidding from closing in on 2 million. It went a little slower, but still relatively quickly considering each increase was now $100,000 a pop. Then, at $2.1 million, it was sold, the largest sum ever paid for Munnings' work. Just afterward, ironically, a portrait of the duchess by Gerald Brockhurst, which we had been told *was* first-rate, fetched just over its high estimate of $90,000.

Soon after the paintings came the books.

The first books were not really books to us. They were volumes that related to Edward or his family. For example, lot number 1344 was an impressively bound blank notebook with the prince of Wales seal on the cover. Lot number 1347 was a beautifully bound inventory of his jewels, and number 1348 was a similar list of his silver.

It was during the bidding for these lots that we noticed a very serious woman in her late thirties wearing glasses in a row just down from where we were sitting. She had bought the Windsors' library pole ladder for $8,000. As soon as the book lots came up, she started bidding on just about everything. Unlike other bidders, who gave only the tiniest surreptitious twitch of their paddle to up the price, this woman held her paddle up in an authoritative way and kept it up until she got what she wanted. In this manner, she bought ten or fifteen lots in the 4,000 and $5,000 range, and not once did she crack a smile or exhibit any change in demeanor. A number of times she outbid dealers we knew in the room, and was rewarded with a glare or a frown, to which she was apparently oblivious. Only once was she outbid herself, and she accepted defeat with the same aplomb with which she had accepted victory. If our days at the auction had taught us anything, it was how to recognize a dealer. And if we had ever seen a dealer bidding for a customer or buying things she knew she could resell, it was this woman.

Finally, it was time for the Churchills. We turned and watched her. Maybe she was the one who was here for Steve Forbes or Bill Gates.

But she never moved. The bidding was mostly on the phones, although there was a man in his sixties in a plaid shirt who hung in until $80,000, then got up and stalked out of the hall when he got taken out. Finally, after some slow and agonized bidding, at least for this auction, someone on the telephone got the Churchills for $130,000. Seventeen lots later, *Profiles in Courage* sold for $36,000, again to a telephone bidder, without the stone-faced woman lifting her paddle.

We were curious both about her and whoever had bought the Churchills, so afterward we asked a Sotheby's press officer. She told us that the Churchills were bought by a man named John McCall—he'd bought *Profiles in Courage,* too—and that the woman, whom we will call Laura D., would not mind speaking to us.

After the session ended, we approached her tentatively. We waited as she finished a conversation with a woman who had been sitting in the row behind her.

"Excuse us. Laura?"

Laura D. jumped and turned around, staring at us, her eyes wide. "What is it?" she asked, as if we were state troopers who had just stopped her for going eighty in a fifty-five zone. "How do you know my name?"

"The press office told us."

"Oh." She blew out a huge sigh and then smiled. "I thought, well . . . they look about my age. Maybe their kids know my kids."

"Uh, no. We were wondering about the books you bought . . ."

"Oh, wasn't it terrific? I got lots of terrific books."

"Which ones did you think were the best?"

"Oh, I don't know. I don't know anything about books. I just thought that they were terrific."

We didn't know quite what to say to this.

"I was bidding a little for myself—I just had to have the library ladder—but mostly for a friend of mine who owns a little antiques shop where I come from. When I told her I was coming to the auction, she said, 'Just get anything you can. This kind of stuff just flies out of my store.' So I just bought her anything I thought she might like. My husband's in advertising. He wanted the garden books . . . the only thing in the whole auction he wanted was the garden books . . . but I was so focused on the other books that I forgot to bid on them. I hope he doesn't get mad at me."

"Why don't you tell him that you tried, but that you stopped bidding when it got to be too much money?"

Laura paused. Obviously, the concept of too much money was a new one for her. "That might work," she said finally, although with a dose of skepticism.

"You bought quite a lot for your friend," we offered. "She must have a successful business."

Suddenly, Laura D.'s smile vanished. She seemed to be doing some quick addition in her head. "Oh yes," she said in a half mumble, reaching for her purse and turning to leave.

It turned out that John McCall, the man who had bought the Churchills, didn't mind talking to us either. He lived in Texas and had his own 800 number.

"This is John."

"Hi, John. This is Nancy Goldstone. I'm with *Biblio* magazine, and I wondered if I could ask you some questions about the set of Churchills you bought at Sotheby's yesterday—"

"What is *Biblio,* Nancy?"

"*Biblio*'s one of those glossy magazines about books and collecting. You know, you can find it on the rack at Barnes and Noble—"

"Never go to Barnes and Noble."

"Well, I suppose you might find it at a used-book store—"

"Actually, been to Barnes and Noble once or twice."

"Well, good, you can get a copy then. I was just wondering what exactly you collect. I mean, do you just collect Churchill, or were you interested in the duke and duchess—"

"I collect everything. I have a lot of books. I think I read somewhere that if you have three of something, you're a collector, so I try never to have three of anything."

"Well, how did you get started?"

"I was at a garage sale once, and I bought some old records with some Churchill speeches on them. Then I was driving somewhere, and I stopped along the way at an antiques store, and it turned out they were worth quite a bit of money."

"How much?"

"Five or six thousand dollars."

"What did you pay for them?"

"Fifty dollars."

"That was a good deal."

"Yes. After that, people started giving me books. My father-in-law gave me a romance novel Churchill wrote—did you know that he wrote romance novels?"

"No."

"Well, he did, when he was very young. I also got a couple of books from another set—*The History of the English-Speaking Peoples.* Then I heard about this set at Sotheby's, and I thought I'd get it."

"Did you inspect the books yourself, or did you just buy them off the catalog?"

"I bought them off the catalog. I meant to go to New York, but something came up here, and I couldn't."

"Was there anything about this particular set that you wanted?"

"Well, they were signed and all—I think the set was worth more because of the historical significance."

"Did you think you got a good price?"

"Well, I was willing to go about thirty thousand dollars higher. I wrote down one hundred and sixty thousand dollars in the book."

"I think you got a good price. There were some dealers in the audience, and they all stopped at eighty thousand. But they usually like to double their investment."

"I pretty much know what things are worth. I've always known what things are worth, I don't know why," said John modestly.

"Did you speak to any dealers about these books before you bought them?'

"No. I have other inscribed books by Churchill, and I know what they're worth, so . . . I bought the *Profiles in Courage,* too."

"I know. Did you also attend the Onassis auction?"

"I have Jackie O's saddle," he said.

"So you're not just a book collector. When did you start collecting?"

"When I was three or four. Collecting's a progressive disease. I have all my old toys."

"You must have a big house."

"I have big warehouses. You know that movie *Citizen Kane*? I keep looking for my little red stool."

"You didn't name it, did you?"

"No, but I watch that movie all the time, and he reminds me of me. I collect lots of things—guns, buttons, books. I actually read the books. I collect them to read them. I have this book by Teddy Roosevelt, it's the last one he wrote, the Brazil book, you know he died of the diseases he got there, malaria and all, anyway, I went out on a hunting trip, and I took that book with me, and I was reading it, and one of my friends said, 'That book's signed by Teddy Roosevelt! What are you doing with it out in the snow?' But that's why I buy them. I think they should be used and read and enjoyed. Same with an antique gun. The nicks are part of it. What do you do, Nancy?"

"I write books and articles."

"Can you make a living at that?"

"Well, you can't have big warehouses, but everybody's got their own tastes."

"What kind of books do you write?"

"I wrote a book about book collecting with my husband, Larry. I also wrote some funny murder mysteries."

"Oh, yeah? Do you know Kinky Friedman?"

"I've heard the name."

"He's on the *New York Times* best-seller list."

"He's doing very well then."

"He put me in one of his books. *Road Kill.* I'm in a chapter at the end."

"I'll look you up. By the way, how would you like me to describe you in the article? As a businessman from Texas?"

"You can call me the Shampoo King from Dripping Springs, Nancy. And if you're ever in Texas, be sure to look me up."

We remembered that Ruth, the book person from Klein's, our local department store, was from Texas and had once said that she had grown up with Kinky Friedman. She even called him Richard. We got her on the phone and asked her if she knew John McCall. She said she couldn't place the name, but when we told her about *Road Kill,* she remembered the character immediately.

"What about Dripping Springs?" we asked. "Is there really such a place?"

"Oh, yeah. It's a charming little town out in the middle of nowhere. Nobody really lives there. It's a place people go to on weekends to get stoned, skinny dip, and make love on the rocks."

"You ever do any of that?"

Ruth paused a moment. "Two out of three," she said.

In addition to this fascinating information about Dripping Springs, we also found out that John McCall's Churchill romance novels might not be exactly what he thought they were.

After the article came out in *Biblio,* a professor emeritus of English at Bellarmine College in Louisville, Kentucky, named Wade Hall sent in a letter to the magazine.

"I enjoyed very much the article by Lawrence and Nancy Goldstone," he began. (We liked him already.) Professor Hall went on to note that:

> I suspect, like a lot of people, McCall confused the American novelist Winston Churchill [1871–1947] with the British soldier, statesman, and historian Winston S. Churchill [1874–1965]. Before World War I, to most Americans *the* Winston Churchill was the one born in St. Louis, Missouri. He had already written some eight novels, including *Richard Carvel* [1899], an immensely successful historical novel . . .
>
> The fictional title character serves during the Revolution under John Paul Jones and is wounded in the naval battle between the *Bonhomme Richard* and the *Serapis.* So successful was Churchill's re-creation of Jones that the navel hero's reputation was enhanced and his body found and removed to the United States for burial.
>
> After the publication of *The Crisis* in 1901, a novel of the American Civil war, Churchill was recognized as one of the nation's foremost novelists . . .
>
> As both [Churchills] were becoming celebrities, the Briton wrote the American and suggested that one of them should modify his name. The American agreed but recommended that the Briton, three years his junior, should

> make the change. The future Sir Winston Churchill thereafter signed himself Winston S. Churchill.
>
> As the Briton's fame increased through the new century, the American writer's reputation waned. At his death in 1947 few people knew who he was.
>
> Apparently, at the end of the century, hardly anyone knows. Remember, however, that those much-read novels you see in yard sales and used book stores were written by the *other* Winston Churchill, the American one.

Finally, it was Tuesday morning, time for session nine and lot number 1767, the literature we were hoping to get. For this session, not only did we not sit in the press area, we brought our daughter, Emily, almost seven years old, to "help Daddy raise the paddle."

We had spent the last several days agonizing over how much we were willing to bid to try and get these books. Even in the best case, we would be spending two or three times more than we had ever spent at one time on books (of course, we would be getting a lot more books than we had ever bought at one time as well.) Although we were still skeptical about the estimated value—$15 apiece for books such as these seemed wildly low—we had allowed ourselves to be convinced that there was actually a chance that this lot might go for somewhere near Sotheby's estimate. We finally decided we'd be willing to spend as much as (gulp) $3,000. That meant that, with the buyer's premium and sales tax, we couldn't bid more than 2,500.

We looked around the room. Good. It was the Friday/Monday crowd, not the weekenders. Maybe we'd have a chance. Then, disaster. There was Laura D. just to the left of us, again stony faced, her catalog open, paddle in her lap. But wait. She wasn't bidding. Not at all. Not even once. And, on closer examination she looked . . . chastened. Apparently her friend with the little antique shop had not been as pleased at having to fork over $50,000 as Laura had assumed she would be.

Our lot came up at the end of the session. "Get ready," we whispered to Emily, who moved closer to Daddy and put her hand on the paddle.

"Lot number 1767, English Literature," began the auctioneer. "We begin the bidding at—"

Emily and Daddy lifted the paddle a few inches off their laps.

"Three thousand dollars," said the auctioneer.

Daddy made Emily put the paddle down.

Within seconds, the bidding was up to $10,000, and the set finally went for $13,000 to someone on the telephone.

FOR IMMEDIATE RELEASE

SOTHEBY'S SALE OF THE COLLECTION OF THE DUKE AND DUCHESS OF WINDSOR TOTALS $23,355,838

—Nine-Day Auction, Longest in American History, Achieves More than Three Times Its Pre-Sale High Estimate.

"We are absolutely thrilled with these outstanding results," said Diana D. Brooks, President and Chief Executive Officer of Sotheby's. "Momentum and excitement built steadily over the nine days of sales, attesting to the enduring legacy of the Duke and Duchess of Windsor and to their unforgettable place in history."

Well, yes, but for a slightly different perspective, there was Emily Goldstone, writing in her first-grade journal. We quote verbatim:

I went to Sathebys. I saw what wuns belonged to the duke and duches of winser. They wer vary selfish people but enyhow they wer rich. Some pepole just wanted to see them cause they wer rich. Cause they wer a duk and duches. They did not care if they wer nice people or not. Me and my family thought that was vary wrong. Espesaly me. The duke used to be king. He was not good. He quited just bafor world two. His brother became king. He was good. His dauter, Elizabth is queen today. I saw pritty dresis and ugly suits.

Chapter 10

"You going to Litchfield?" Kevin Rita asked us one day in early March.

"What's in Litchfield?"

"The fair. Oh, you've got to go. It's one of the best."

There seem to be a lot more small regional book fairs around these days. You'd think that would be good news—plenty of opportunities to see good books in quiet rural settings with no big city traffic to brave, no $15 parking lots, no $10 entrance fees, and no $8.95 fruit salad. Unfortunately, all too many regional fairs are held in underlit and overheated halls, with dealers crammed together like rush-hour passengers on the Tokyo subway and aisle space that would be inadequate for Jack Sprat. There also tends to be an overrepresentation of surly, grumbling booksellers with not especially interesting books at vastly inflated prices, whose main topic of conversation is what a pain it was to get there and how much it cost for the booth and now he's not even selling any books. That is often followed by an accusing glare in your direction, the meaning of which is obvious.

But if Kevin told us that the Litchfield Book Fair was special . . .

"Sure," we said. "We'll take a shot."

The town of Litchfield is in the county of Litchfield, which covers the entire northwest corner of Connecticut. Although the county does include Torrington, it is otherwise largely rural, dotted with the kind of adorable New England towns that seem to be irresistible to celebrities. Dustin Hoffman has a home there, as does Arthur Miller. The Buckley family, as in William F., has made its country home in nearby Sharon for generations.

The fair was being held at Wamogo High School. Regional book fairs are often held at schools, although they are rarely named "Wamogo." It sounded like the name of the nonsensical disease "Mogo-on-the-Gagogo" that W. C. Fields made up in *The Bank Dick*. The school itself was a red-brick institutional building, the poor relation of Litchfield High School just up the road. As we drove in, a man of about eighty in a maroon V-neck sweater with a golf hat tilted rakishly on his head nodded ever so slightly to direct us to a parking spot.

Directly inside the door, near the desk that had been set up to sell the $3 admission tickets, we saw a sign:

> There was a mix-up by
> the school and a basketball
> tournament was scheduled
> at the same time as the fair.
> Please bear with us. We
> will do all we can to keep
> the two events apart.
>
> Nutmeg books

Forcing down visions of dodging flying basketballs, we paid our $6 and walked in.

As we moved into the main hall, we noticed banners on the walls that read: BELIEVE IN YOURSELF! and NEVER NEVER QUIT!

We assumed we were in the gym, which was odd considering the basketball tournament, but it turned out to be the cafeteria.

Although the room was set up in the standard manner, with booths ringing the walls and aisles in the center of the room, the aisles were wider than at most fairs, so we didn't have to elbow our way past other collectors in order to see the books. The extra space also served to absorb the sound and the heat, imparting an immediate air of relaxation.

It was only ten-thirty in the morning, but the room was already filled with customers moving about. It was an attractive, well-groomed crowd and a good deal more courteous than we were used to. Still, this *was* a book fair, and thus it attracted the usual contingent of eccentrics. One short man in a raincoat (it was clear and eighty degrees outside) went from booth to booth, going up to each dealer and asking, "Do you have anything about roses?" He must have made the rounds more than once because when he walked up to one booth, the dealer pointed at him before he could open his mouth and said, "I know. Roses." Also in the crowd were a number of dealers who had come to buy, rather than to sell, books, which is always a good sign.

Of those who did come to sell, there were several dealers we knew. John Sanderson had his usual collection of obscure and eclectic titles. For a sweet, learned, rather shy man, he certainly has extreme taste in nonfiction. We saw *The Lunacy Acts, The Law Relating to Lunacy, Alcohol Addiction and Chronic Alcoholism,* and *The Disorder of Speech,* one after another on his shelves.

"Been out on the golf course?" we asked.

"Not yet this year," John replied with a small shrug. Then he gave a quick, furtive glance around to see if anyone was listening. "Maybe this afternoon after the fair."

Esther and David Kininmonth, old friends of ours from Berkshire Book Company, had a first of *The Shuttered Room & Other Stories* for $135, and *Cecil Beaton's New York* in an arresting dust jacket for $90. Also on their shelves were *Clothes and the Horse: A Guide to Correct Dress for All Riding Occasions* and *Tobacco Leaf,* which was a treatise on how to grow tobacco in Connecticut. Business must have been good because they noted with great satisfaction that they were off to Paris in a few weeks.

Just past the entrance, in the hall where about ten other booths were set up, was a sign that read, GARY WHITE, BOOKSELLER. We had never heard of Gary White before, so we stopped to take a look. There were some modern firsts, children's books including an illustrated copy of *Hans Brinker or The Silver Skates,* and coffee-table books like *Musical Instruments Through the Ages.* Most of the books were in good condition, and none were overpriced. In fact, he had a first-edition, first state of *For Whom the Bell Tolls* for only $175. We knew this to be a book that regularly sold elsewhere for in excess of $250, often in not nearly as good condition as was this one.

"Well, the dust jacket is slightly chipped at the top of the spine," Gary explained.

The dust jacket did have a small chip at the top of the spine, but still, $175 was a great price. We noticed from his card that Gary was from Montrose, New York, which wasn't far from us, so we struck up a conversation. We began, as we usually do, by handing him the book we were going to buy, in this case *Hans Brinker,* and asking him how he got into the business.

"It started with boxing books," said Gary. He appeared to be in his forties, lean, with unusually good posture and was a good deal more fit-looking than most book dealers. "I collected baseball cards, and on the back of one of the cards, I saw a question on boxing that I wasn't sure of . . . who won the fight in 1910 in Reno, Nevada, between Jack Johnson and Jim Jefferies. So I went to the local bookstore to look for a book on boxing, and I couldn't find any. Finally, I found some books in the library. After I took them out, I realized that I *really* didn't want to take them back." He was holding his hands like the books were still in them. "I did, of course . . . but I didn't want to. So I started going around buying boxing books.

"Then one day about ten years ago, I saw a book . . . it wasn't about boxing, and I wasn't really interested in it, but I knew it was worth a lot more than it was selling for, so I bought it and then sold it. That's when I started being in the business."

"Do you have a shop?" we asked, offering him our credit card.

"I don't take credit cards," he said, shaking his head. "I don't have a shop, and I don't work off the Internet either. It's too much of a hassle. I do this just for fun."

"So you have another job then?"

He nodded. "I'm a piano mover."

At the far end of the hall, we saw Margaret O'Connell of Tenney River Books. Although her books were interesting, it was hard not to notice a sign printed in bright red letters, sitting to the left of her case. It read:

TEAMSTERS
LOCAL 653 ON
STRIKE
UPS UNFAIR

"This is the third fair I've brought it to," she said. "Each time before, a UPS guy walked up and growled at me, 'I've got one of those at home, and *I'm* not gonna sell it.' "

"What do you want for it?"

"Seven dollars and fifty cents," she replied.

Kevin Rita had a booth, too, of course. He had brought *English Cooking, Fois Gras and Trumpets,* and *The Viscomte in the Kitchen.* There were also *Bloomsbury Reflections*; Vita Sackville-West's *Garden Book,* and *A Childhood in Brittany Eighty Years Ago* by Anne Douglas Sedgwick. He also had a pristine first edition of *A Night to Remember,* probably the best book ever on the *Titanic* (and made into by far the best movie), at the special post-Oscar price of $250.

"How's Snagsby?" we asked.

Kevin's brow darkened. "He's fine but he's been temporarily banished from the store."

"Why?" we asked.

He barked at a customer and he threw up," said Kevin.

Seeing note-taking in progress, a complete stranger walked up to us. "Write down it's the lure of the hunt," he said. His name was Gerald, and he was there from Torrington with his wife. Gerald handed us a business card that noted that he was the head of a financial-services company. It must be a testament to the times and to Torrington that in addition to Title 19 planning, tax returns, and bookkeeping, one of the services Gerald offered was divorce mediation.

"What?" we asked.

"The lure of the hunt," Gerald repeated. "That's why people come to these things. We go to book fairs often."

"How would you rate this one?"

"Oh, this is a very good one," said Gerald.

"Why do you think so?"

"Because there are lots of interesting books in very good shape," he replied, using the tone of a person explaining why it is hot in the summer and cold in the winter.

Never let it be said that when we go someplace, we don't do our research.

The Litchfield Book Fair has been going on for sixteen years, "and each year we learn something new," said Debbie Goring, who, with her husband Bill, runs Nutmeg Books, which sponsored the fair.

"We noticed that there was no book fair for Connecticut dealers," said Bill, "so we started out just inviting dealers within the state. We did well, and pretty soon dealers started coming from all over the area.

"The secret of a good fair," he added, "is to think about the dealers."

"It's the little things," said Debbie. "Provide coffee when they're setting up and maybe some doughnuts. It's a big job . . .

packing, loading, unloading, setting up . . . a little recognition of all the trouble they took to come here goes a long way. This way, even if they don't sell as much as they'd hoped to, they can have a pretty good time."

"We hold the fair at the end of March," said Bill, "because early spring is a time when a lot of dealers have been in all winter and have good books to sell. Also, we only hold it once a year, not twice. That way people always look forward to it."

Unlike other fairs, where just about any dealer who pays for a booth can get one, the Gorings are more restrictive.

"I do the layout," said Debbie, "and I make sure that there is room to move, so that there is a flow and people will have easy access to all the booths. That means that we strictly limit the number of booths we'll have. It's better to have a smaller fair that works than a biger one that doesn't."

There were forty-two dealers at this fair, although, according to Bill, "We could fill over twenty more booths from the waiting list if we wanted to." But the most unusual thing about the Litchfield fair is not the limit on the quantity of dealers, but the restrictions on the quality.

"We don't take people from the waiting list on a first-come-first-serve basis," said Bill. "We get kind of a committee together and try to see which dealer on the list will keep a good balance.

"If we lose a dealer in modern firsts who has relatively expensive books, we're not going to replace him with someone who does sporting books, or even a dealer who does cheap modern firsts. We want to represent as many ranges of interest and price as we can and still keep the fair interesting. We've got some dealers who've been on the waiting list for years that we'd love to have, but we just can't fit them in."

There is one other criterion of admission.

"Most of all, we want all the dealers at this fair to be of a certain quality," said Debbie. "We don't take dealers who have shabby-looking books or are shabby looking themselves. Most of all, we want people who get along well with customers and other dealers."

"No schmucks," Bill added succinctly.

Although the Gorings probably did not do this on purpose, it is also a very good idea to hold a book fair in a place that has a good restaurant nearby. We confess that in this case, it was not just Kevin Rita's enthusiasm that had brought us to Litchfield. It was also the opportunity to stop for lunch at the West Street Grill.

The West Street Grill is opposite the village green in the center of town, amid three-story white-clapboard homes with gingerbread roofs, solid-looking red-brick colonials, and steepled church spires that comfortably coexist with gourmet food and wine shops, antique dealers, and Talbots.

The restaurant has been open for eight years and in that time has been featured in everything from the *New York Times* to *Bon Appetit* to *Playboy*. As with Rick's in Casablanca, everyone goes to the West Street Grill. Arthur Miller eats there. Philip Roth eats there. William Styron eats there. And once before, just after they opened, the Goldstones had eaten there.

On the recommendation of friends, we had met at the West Street Grill for dinner. The food had been extraordinary, the wine perfect, the ambience casually elegant, and the bill of sufficient size that we had not been back there since.

But, in fine restaurants, for people like us, lunch is the ticket. The food is the same, but the prices aren't.

The main room of the West Street Grill is long and narrow, with black-fabric benches and black tables and black mirrors on one wall and a painted mural of a sky—the bottom nine inches is dark green horizon, the rest is solid blue—along the other. It was a Sunday, just after noon, when restaurants can begin to serve alcohol with brunch, so we got there just as the place was starting to fill up and got a table right away.

At the time, we thought we would be doing an article about the Litchfield fair. As we sat down we noticed two men standing and talking by the bar who were clearly not customers. One of us had an idea.

"Hey, I'll bet those are the owners. Let's talk to them, and put the restaurant in the article."

"Okay, Larry, but let's have lunch first."

"No. I'm going to introduce myself now. They might not be here after lunch."

"Please don't. You always embarrass me."

Moments later:

"What did they say, Larry?"

"They said, sure. See, you didn't have to worry. They said, eat lunch, and then we'll talk afterward."

The waiter came over a few seconds later. We ordered a glass of wine each and one of us ordered the Goat Cheese and Roasted Tomato Omelette with Steak Fries and Toast Points and the other the Curried Dusted Codfish Sandwich with Red Pepper Aioli on Foccaccio with Shoe String Fries and Cumin Scented Bean Salad.

We handed over the menus, and the wine came immediately. It was chilled, crisp, and dry. Just as we had finished toasting to a civilized afternoon in the country, the waiter reappeared and placed a cup of soup in front of each of us.

"This is the special Roasted Sweet Corn and Apple Chowder," he began.

"No, no," we said. "We didn't order any soup."

"Charles wanted you to try this," said the waiter.

"Oh. Please thank him for us."

We tasted the soup. It is probably trite to say that this was the best soup we'd ever had in our lives, but it was the best soup we'd ever had in our lives.

We finished the soup and continued sipping our wine. The afternoon was getting more pleasant by the moment.

The soup cups were whisked away, and one of the two men from the bar appeared at the table bearing a plate. With him was a dark, good-looking man of about thirty, wearing a wild, multicolored batik shirt and a dark brimless hat that made him look like a cross between an African tribal leader and a Polish rabbinical student.

"Hello, Nancy," said the man from the bar. "I already met your husband. I'm Charles Kafferman, one of the owners." Charles was in his fifties, tan and prosperous looking, wearing pressed jeans and a country shirt. "I'd like to introduce you to our chef, Robert Timan."

The man in the batik shirt shook our hands. Charles put the plate on the table.

"I'd like you both to try this," he said. "This is one of our specialities. We're known for this."

It was some kind of hot cheesey bread, and there was a lot of it on the plate. We each tried a slice.

"Wow. This is *great,*" we said.

"Yes, it is, isn't it?" said Charles with obvious pride. "It's Grilled Peasant Bread with Parmesan Aioli. We've been written up for this." He paused. "Okay, I'll leave you to enjoy your lunch now. We can speak after."

Charles and Robert left. Within minutes, we had polished off the entire plate of bread. We were filling up fast, when the waiter arrived with our entrées. They didn't last long either.

The waiter took our empty plates. Each of us, feeling like Jabba the Hut, leaned back in our chairs and held our stomachs.

But then the waiter appeared once more. "Charles wanted you to try the Dark Chocolate Sorbet," he said placing two flutes filled with delectable dark brown stuff on the table.

What the hell, if Charles wanted it . . .

"I wanted to give people a really good country American restaurant," said Jim O'Shea, the other owner, as we sat in the back and talked. It seemed a funny ambition for someone who was raised in Ireland. Jim is a restauranteur and cooking teacher, which is fortunate because Charles, as it turns out, used to be in the garment center.

"It's what you're looking for in the country," Jim went on. "Casual yet formal. Sophisticated. I wanted the interior to be simple, minimalist, but also have a sense of history in mind. I just washed the floor down, stripped it completely, and then painted huge diamonds on it, so it looks like it's been here a long time.

"Litchfield is more of a weekend neighborhood place," he said. "It's not really summer people, and I wanted the restaurant to reflect that. As for the food, I looked for a young chef who wasn't recognized and worked with him on the concept. We've had a couple of chefs since but the concept has always remained the same."

Whatever Jim's concept was, it was fine with us.

We thanked Jim and Charles and paid the bill. They had charged us for what we had ordered, the entrées and the wine, but not for all the goodies Charles had dropped off at the table.

It was very quiet on the ride home.

Finally: "Nancy?"

"Hmm?"

"That was fun, wasn't it?"

"Yeah."

"Great fair."

"Uh-huh."

"Terrific food, too."

"Terrific."

There was a few seconds pause.

"Nancy?"

"Hmm?"

"Do you think we should do food next?"

"I don't think our stomachs could take it."

"Yeah, I suppose . . ."

So we just sat there contentedly and let the miles float by, our distended bellies in the front, our newly purchased books in the back.